Praise for *Finders Keepers:*

"Not only does Bowden do a bang-up job relating the raw facts, he plunges headlong into the ethical quicksand that can swallow people confronted by large sums of cash. . . . [Joey Coyle's] eventual fate is a sadly logical conclusion to this modern-day fable of self-destruction, greed and moral vacuity."
—Donna Marchetti, *The Plain Dealer* (Cleveland)

"A brisk, sad story . . . [As Bowden] accurately reports, South Philly is a close-knit clump of ethnic neighborhoods."
—Anthony Day, *Los Angeles Times*

"Bowden's writing is razor-sharp; you come away from his fast-paced narrative convinced he understands Joey better than he's willing to admit. Perhaps we all do." —Elaine Margolin, *San Francisco Chronicle*

"Rich . . . *Finders Keepers* is not your standard adventure tale, but it has the same kind of edge and steam-rolling pacing as the rest of that genre. . . . A classic story line, and Bowden makes the most of it."
—*National Geographic Adventure*

"You find yourself cheering for Joey Coyle, the urban folklore hero of *Finders Keepers.* . . . [Bowden's] prolific use of dialogue—short, snappy sentences with a South Philly accent—keep the story lively and moving along in this quick read, perfect for an airline trip. . . . Bowden also paints scenes that leave you chuckling."
—Lynn Bronikowski, *Rocky Mountain News*

"*Finders Keepers* retains the rumpled charm and snappy pace of good beat reporting. . . . Bowden has delivered a story of parable-like clarity and timelessness." —Paul Collins, *Oregonian*

"[Bowden] presents Joey Coyle's story sympathetically, but without whitewashing the facts." —L. D. Meagher, CNN.com

"Funny, sad and exasperating." —Jim Clark, *Columbus Dispatch*

"A master at pacing, putting the reader right alongside Joey, feeling the same speed-induced high as he makes dumb and dumber decisions...Most of all, Mr. Bowden leaves the reader pondering the most obvious question on each page: What would you do?" —Todd Wills, *Dallas Morning News*

"[A] fast reading account of a fool and his money. Bowden keeps a low and nonjudgmental profile but doles out his account like a good storyteller. It's testament to his solid narrative that even long after the sad sack Coyle loses his charm, his story maintains our interest." —*The Tampa Tribune*

"An interesting crime story . . . [*Finders Keepers*] does such a good job documenting human nature, both generous and selfish." —James Hart, *The Kansas City Star*

"An amazing-but-true tale . . . In fiction Coyle would wind up on a tropical isle, but the real tragicomic ending is still compelling, if only because it happened to some other schmuck." —Laurina Gibbs, *Maxim*

"[This] mesmerizing—and tragic—fable is a worst-case illustration of 'Be careful what you wish for.'" —*Details*

"An interesting portrait of a desperate man who learns that a $1.2 million windfall—one that literally fell off a truck—wasn't the answer to his prayers." —Mark Skoneki, *Orlando Sentinel*

"Provocative . . . A sobering lesson about the dark side of human nature . . . Bowden has a knack for finding that peculiar, little told news story and turning it into a full-blown narrative that makes the literary world sit up and take notice." —Mark Davis, *The Daytona Beach News-Journal*

"[Bowden] documents both the story and its characters with clarity and riveting suspense. . . . [*Finders Keepers*] reflects true reporting at its very best." —Larry Cox, *The Tucson Citizen*

FINDERS

KEEPERS

Also by Mark Bowden:

Doctor Dealer

Bringing the Heat

Black Hawk Down

Killing Pablo

FINDERS

KEEPERS

THE STORY OF A MAN WHO
FOUND $1 MILLION

MARK BOWDEN

Grove Press / *New York*

Portions of this book originally appeared in *The Philadelphia Inquirer Sunday Magazine.*

Published simultaneously in Canada
Printed in the United States of America

FIRST GROVE PRESS EDITION

Library of Congress Cataloging-in-Publication Data
Bowden, Mark, 1951-
Finders keepers : the story of a man who found $1 million / Mark Bowden.
p. cm.
ISBN 0-8021-4021-1 (pbk.)
1. Coyle, Joey. 2. Stevedores—Pennsylvania—Philadelphia—Biography. 3. Narcotic addicts—Pennsylvania—Philadelphia—Biography. 4. Working class—Pennsylvania—Philadelphia. 5. Theft. 6. Philadelphia (Pa.)—Biography. I. Title.
CT275.C8647 B69 2002
974.8'11'092—dc21
[B]   2002066712

Design by Laura Hammond Hough

Grove Press
841 Broadway
New York, NY 10003

03   04   05   06   07   10 9 8 7 6 5 4 3 2 1

To Rhoda Weyr

CONTENTS

There is an old expression in South Philly for anything of uncertain origin. They say, "It fell off the truck."

It means: *Don't ask.*

DAY ONE

Thursday
February 26, 1981

1

Joey Coyle was crashing. He had been high all night, and coming down from the meth always made him feel desperate and confused. When he was cranked up the drug gave him gusts of energy so great that his lungs and brain fought to keep pace. That was how he felt at night. When he slept it was usually during the day.

Today there would be little sleep because he had used up his whole stash. No stash and, as usual, no money. It had been almost a month since the union had called to give him work on the docks. He made good money as a longshoreman. It was where his father had worked and where his older brother worked. Joey had never finished high school but he had an educated feel for machinery. On the docks they used him to repair the lifts, and he was good at it. He took pride in that. Engine grease colored gray the heavy calluses on his hands. But for more than a year the economy had been bad in Philadelphia and there had been few chances to work. They had called him to fill in for a few weeks over the Christmas holidays, but there had been nothing since. So the desperation kicked in at sunrise. Where would he find the next fix?

The empty hours weighed on Joey. He was twenty-eight and he still lived in his mother's house. He was devoted to his mom. His father had died of a heart attack on a night after Joey had stormed out following an argument. The old man hadn't liked the length of Joey's hair. His last words to his son were spoken in anger, and Joey believed he had killed him. Eight years had passed and the guilt he felt was undiminished. Looking after his mother had helped, staying with her, but she had fallen ill with liver disease and she needed care he couldn't give, or couldn't be relied upon to give. She had moved just a few blocks away to his sister Ellen's apartment. Joey took it as another defeat. He felt like he had let his mother down, but also that she had let *him* down. She had left. He felt rejected and a failure, but would not have put those words on the feelings because Joey was not the type to look inside himself to figure out how and why he felt the way he did. He just kept moving. Meth helped with that. Most people called it speed. Joey called it "blow." It blew away all the demons of self-doubt and depression. In the months since his mother left his days blurred into nights in a speeding carousel of exhilarating highs and then crushing lows. Then would come the accelerating frantic urge to find money to buy more, to fire himself up again.

His home on Front Street was at the tattered edge of the tight matrix of South Philly's streets. To the west was the neighborhood's strong, nurturing core, its churches, schools, markets, and corner restaurants and bars. It was the oldest part of the city, low houses in row after brick row, most of them just two stories high. Kinship was sewn tightly in its even blocks.

Brothers lived across narrow streets from brothers, fathers from sons and nephews and grandsons. In the narrow alleys folks would grin at the way they could sometimes see in the awkward way a boy ran or squinted or threw a ball the reflected image of his grandfather or great-uncle. When a man from South Philly said he knew a fellow "from the neighborhood," it meant something more like family than an acquaintance. South Philly was Catholic. It was proud and superstitious, pragmatic and devout.

The world had changed around South Philly. The jobs that had built it were mostly gone. It cohered like a fine-spun rug, its loyalties and affections knit tougher than the forces that would wear it down. It was a shelter against change, the future. Out Joey's back door, to the east, was a vision of the unforgiving world outside its boundaries, a wasteland, a vast expanse of weedy, trash-piled lots, junkyards, old brick warehouses defaced with graffiti, the discarded remnants of a once thriving port and manufacturing giant. Rusting hulks of old boxcars crouched in forlorn rows alongside the newer cars that occasionally came and went, moving between the fenced-in lots around the trucking yards and dwindling industrial works along the Delaware River waterfront. Over this bleak expanse the air was tinged gray and tasted of ash. Just behind the row of houses on Joey's block loomed the hulking concrete underside of Interstate 95, which cast a perpetual shadow wider than a city block.

When Joey was a little boy he would leave the comfortable nest of his neighborhood to play in the wasteland. He would pass through the cool shadow of the interstate, with its incessant traffic overhead roaring like an angry god. He would search out clusters of rat holes, pour gasoline down them, and set them on fire. He would leave one hole dry, then sit a few yards away from it to shoot at the fleeing rats with a bow and arrow. When he was older, he and his friends stealthily passed TV sets from loaded boxcars to waiting arms, then ran to trade the loot for money to buy grass and beer. For a boy, and then a young man, the wasteland was a haven, a place to escape all the friendly watching eyes of the neighborhood. It was wild, exciting, and even dangerous. Once older bullies had knocked him around and hung him by his thumbs. So long as you had your friends to help you down and you could come back every night to your mom and dad, your house, your block, the world outside was mostly a thrill. But now it just loomed.

Unlike his old friends, Joey had not outgrown those years. The death of his father, the decline of the shipyards, his growing dependency on the drug—it all conspired to prolong his childhood. Born in a different age, Joey might have lived his life happily along a well-worn path, to work after high school, marriage, children, grandfatherhood, and gone to his eternal rest in Holy Cross Cemetery. But the jobs were gone. Most of Joey's friends had gone to school and learned skills and found work elsewhere, but Joey couldn't adapt. He lacked the patience to sit still in school and to read a book. He had to be moving, doing. That's why he liked working on the docks, where he could learn on his feet, using his hands. Without the work, he was just stuck.

Still, despite his demons, he was feckless and fun loving in a way that endeared him to those who loved him. His complexion was pale pink, his hair so thin and blond you could hardly make out the mustache he had been growing for five years or the eyebrows over his small, deep-set pale blue eyes. Joey spoke in a gruff whisper that often turned into laughter. He had the generosity of a child who doesn't yet understand the value of things. If Joey was in the mood, he would give you anything, even things that didn't belong to him. It was easy to like him, but also easy to be frustrated by him, because you couldn't count on Joey for anything. His word was as insubstantial as the breath it took to give it.

Trouble was immune to Joey's charm; it sought him out and when it stayed away he went looking for it. Like the time his car stalled and blocked a street. Now, blocking streets is a time-honored privilege in South Philly, a way the locals assert turf. With cars parked on both sides of a narrow street, there was often only one lane to work with. But it was understood that passage on these streets was at the pleasure of those who lived there. If somebody from down the street wanted to stop his car and have a chat with a neighbor on a stoop, well, traffic behind him could just wait. If you had groceries to take into the house, you stopped your car on the street in front of your door and delivered the goods. The day Joey's car stalled, he got out to take a look under the hood. A man in a car trapped behind him, clearly ignorant of neighborhood protocol, disputed the blockade. Joey grew indignant, and in the ensuing brawl the stranger drew a savage slice across the left side of Joey's face. It had healed into a crooked gray scar from eye to earlobe. There was nothing funny about that scar but Joey would tell the story in a way that would make you laugh, about how he finally got the man down just in time for the fuzz to arrive and spot him as the aggressor—which earned him another, official, beating. But bad luck just seemed to bounce off Joey. He would laugh and laugh even though the joke was on him. With bitter irony he would call it the luck of the Irish; he even had the word "Irish" tattooed on his upper right arm with a pipe and shamrock and shillelagh. His neck and chest and arms were broad and thick, and his hands seemed oversized, so swollen from all the times he had broken them working on engines that it was hard for him to close them into a fist. He looked tough, especially with that scar, and he had a swagger that went along with it, but he was always more of a danger to himself than to anyone else. Speed had muddied his mind so that sometimes he couldn't think straight for more than a few sentences. His front teeth had all been knocked out and replaced by a row of fakes. When he removed them his face caved in like an old man's. He had the look of someone who had been knocked down a lot on hard streets, yet he had a smile that wouldn't quit.

He would need that resilience for the joke fate would play on him this day.

2

Joey woke up well after noon in his mother's big bed in the wood-paneled bedroom one story above Front Street. He was still slightly high but the urge was gaining on him.

He rose and walked downstairs in his underpants to start a pot of coffee. He went back upstairs while the coffee was brewing and returned wearing worn jeans and a flannel shirt. He poured a cup of black coffee and walked outside to drink it sitting on his front steps. It was a cold afternoon. Joey cupped the coffee in his big hands and scanned the line of parked cars toward Spite's Bar at the corner.

Above the telephone lines that draped lazily across the street the sky was bright gray. He was watching for the mailman. His paycheck for the holiday work was supposed to arrive that day—about $700. That would see him through for a while. But there was no sign of the mailman yet, and even if the check came it would be a hassle getting it cashed. The creeping sick feeling wouldn't wait. Joey decided he would have to beg his dealer to front him the drugs.

Mark Bowden

A few houses down, John Behlau was out working on his
father's car. It was a maroon boat of a Chevy, a '71 Malibu.
Johnny had hammered the right front end of the car back into
shape, and was applying a coat of blue primer. His friend Jed
Pennock was just hanging out, watching him work. Both John
and Jed, like Joey, were unemployed. John was twenty-one. He
was the taller of the two, a skinny, blond-haired kid with a
cocky, tough manner. Jed was short and stout. He had dark hair,
which enabled him, at twenty, to sport a heavier mustache than
Joey. Jed wore glasses with heavy, dark frames, and was, in contrast to his friend, introverted, mild and unsure of himself. Both
young men were stuck in the same rut as Joey, too old for high
school and disinterested in college. They were waiting long, idle
days for the economy to improve so they could get regular work
on the waterfront and resume a normal life.

Joey knew them just as kids in the neighborhood. He was
going to make their day. He walked down and greeted them
with an inviting grin.

"I can cop some blow if you give me ride," he said. Bore-
dom being easy prey to controlled substances, the three set out
at once in the Chevy.

The dealer wasn't in. John and Jed sat in the car while Joey
knocked, paced the sidewalk in front of the house, and then
knocked some more. For the boys it was a minor disappoint-
ment, but they could see that it was more serious with Joey.
He was frantic. He slumped back into the car.

"We can try him again later," he said.

On the way home John stopped to buy gas at the Shell station on Oregon Avenue. Then he took a shortcut home up Swanson Street. It was a bumpy back road through the western edge of the wasteland that ran parallel to the underside of the interstate. Swanson Street had been surrounded by a neighborhood years ago, but the construction of the expressway had left it stranded. It hadn't been repaved for nearly a half century. It now served only as an axle-jarring shortcut for trucks passing from waterfront loading docks to Oregon and Delaware Avenues. For those in the neighborhood it was just a way to avoid the traffic light up at Lee Street. High in the distance to the south was the long approach ramp of the Walt Whitman Bridge.

As John turned up this rugged back route, Joey slumped in the front passenger seat, depressed as the landscape. To the left were familiar mounds of black earth piled with tires, garbage, bedsprings, soggy stained mattresses, and broken glass. To the right was the double fencing around the Purolator Armored Car Company grounds. It was habit for Joe to scan the curbs along Swanson. It was amazing the things you could find. Sometimes people dumped things he could sell or use.

Sure enough, up ahead toward the right curb was a yellow metal tub with its wheels pointing up. John had to slow down to steer the car around it.

"Stop," said Joey. "It might make a good toolbox."

John stopped.

Joey opened the car door and leaned out to right the tub and take a better look at it. It had two lid flaps that joined at the center with holes for padlocks, but there were no padlocks, and as he pushed the tub upright the top fell open. Out on the street spilled two big white canvas bags. Joey pulled one of the bags into the front seat and took a better look at it. It had a lead seal and yellow tag at the top. Black letters on the side spelled out "Federal Reserve Bank."

Joey whooped.

"Holy shit!" he said. "To hell with the box!"

Joey stepped back out to the street and hefted the second bag into the backseat. He slammed that door shut and jumped in front with the first bag.

"Let's get out of here!" he shouted. "Move it! Let's roll!"

"Where?" shouted John, who already had the car moving.

"My house! Go!"

John floored it. The car flew over the railroad tracks and he turned left on Wolf Street. Joey looked for something to tear open the bag. John had a ballpoint pen stuck into the dashboard. Joey pulled it out, poked a hole through the thick canvas of one bag, and tore it open. Then he screamed.

John stopped the car momentarily by the curb between two warehouses to have a look. Jed leaned over the front seat. Inside the torn bag on Joe's lap were tightly wrapped cellophane bundles of what looked like . . . Sweet Jesus! . . . hundred-dollar bills!

"Oh, man!" said Joey. "What am I into now?"

John and Jed whooped deliriously.

Wheels squealed as the Malibu sped into the familiar shadow of I-95. Joey felt a rush like the jolt of a drug. The boys were shouting for joy and thumping him on the shoulders. He just stared at the money and shook with laughter. Joey laughed and laughed. He laughed so hard that the plate with his front teeth plopped into his lap.

3

Rumpled, steady Detective Pat Laurenzi was in his car at about 3 P.M. when he heard the report on his police radio. An armored car had dropped a bag of money somewhere near the vicinity of Front Street near the Purolator Armored Car Company property. No information on the amount missing.

The detective looked like an overgrown kid. He had wide brown eyes and an openness to his face that belied his years in the police department. He liked surprising people who thought he was about ten years younger than his thirty-one years. He wore his straight brown hair cropped in a line high across the middle of his forehead, a real do-it-yourself job. He had made detective five years ago, and he loved his work. When he was on a case that grabbed him, which was most of the time, he would sometimes work straight through days and nights without going home. Who had time for a haircut? Pat sometimes would curl up and sleep right in his car, or wherever, and with the dark patches under his eyes and his hair sticking up in places in back, he often looked like he had just been shaken out of a nap. Some of the detectives in South Philly were dapper. As soon as they got their gold badge they started frequenting the tailors and bought those slipperlike shoes of Italian leather. Not Pat. He dressed like a high school kid late for school. His tight stretch sport shirt was tucked into the belt of light brown jeans, which he pulled high. Beneath his worn gray docksiders he wore white socks.

Returning from a routine chore at police headquarters, Pat was not surprised by the Purolator report. This sort of thing had happened before. It usually involved a couple of thousand dollars and the money usually didn't stay missing long. Along with the missing money there was usually a missing driver, who would show up a few days later hungover and broke in Atlantic City.

Yet as soon as he stepped into his South Philly precinct, a bulky gray stone fortress on a rare tree-lined block, Pat learned immediately that this Purolator drop was far more serious. There had been two metal tubs in the back end of the armored car that afternoon, one with two money bags, the other empty. Both were missing. The company said the bags held a total of $1.2 million. And it was casino money, which meant that instead of the bills being in numerical sequence, the way it comes from the Federal Reserve Bank, these were bundles of random $100 bills, untraceable, the cleanest money money could buy.

With four other detectives and Lieutenant Jimmy Potocnak, Pat drove over to the Purolator building. The company executives there were happy to see them and confided immediately that they suspected the drivers.

"There's just no way the tubs could get out of that truck with both doors closed and locked," one said. "It's impossible."

The company guys wanted the police to give the drivers lie detector tests.

Poor Bill Proctor and Ralph Saracino already knew they were in deep trouble. When he was ushered into a room with the men, Pat could see that Proctor was visibly shaken. He was a middle-aged man with white hair and a bushy mustache, a veteran with the company. He knew at the very least that this fuckup would cost him his job, and he knew that everyone suspected him of stealing the money, or of helping someone else steal it. He had told his story over and over in the past two hours. He swore he had locked the truck doors tightly that afternoon. He had placed the two money bags in one of two empty tubs on wheels that they were supposed to take down to Ventnor, New Jersey, the next day. Saracino, Proctor's younger partner, said that he had watched Proctor fasten the door. They had driven down Delaware Avenue, turned right on Wolf Street, and then left on Swanson down to the back entrance of Purolator. It was a trip they could make blindfolded. It took only about six minutes. Sure, the roads were bad and it had been a bouncy ride, but with the doors locked it couldn't have dropped out!

A dispatcher at the second, interior gate into the company yard had first called their attention to the open door. Proctor had bounded out to see. The steel bars of the right door were still in the locked position, but the door had somehow swung open. Proctor had leaned in the back end to look. Both tubs were gone! He had run back to the front of the truck.

"Turn around," he had shouted to Saracino. "We got to go back and retrace our route!"

Proctor ran back to ask the guard to reopen the first gate. Saracino had then backed the truck out, and Proctor had jumped back in. Their panic eased briefly when they immediately saw a yellow tub up the street. There was no sign of the second tub. Two men were standing over the one. But as they approached the two men, one asked, "Was there anything in this?"

"There *was*," said Proctor, his hopes dashed.

Inside the tub was the yellow receipt for two bags, one carrying $800,000, the other $400,000. There was nothing to say. They had driven past that same spot less than three minutes ago! Somehow, in the time it had taken them to drive a hundred yards, pull through the first Purolator gate, discover the door was open, back out, and return, somebody had removed the bags from the tub. Proctor felt like someone had knocked the air out of him. He felt sick and nervous, and scared.

Everybody had listened to his story with patience but with obvious suspicion. Pat doubted the drivers were telling the truth. The company executives pulled the detectives aside and shook their heads knowingly.

"There's no way," they kept saying. They wanted the lie detector tests. Pat didn't believe in the machine, but he agreed to set the tests up. He asked Proctor and Saracino if they would agree to take it. Both men were alarmed but promptly consented.

As all this was going on, the FBI showed up. They introduced themselves and then just . . . hovered. Given that the money had come from the Federal Reserve Bank, this was going to be one of those instances Pat had heard about but never experienced, where the feds would be "standing by" or "following the case closely" or positioning themselves to be "ready to provide assistance" to local police. The men in suits stood nearby, observing but not commenting or getting involved. It began to get on the Philadelphia detectives' nerves. Pat suspected the feds were probably good at what they did, and with his Cardinal Dougherty High School/Philadelphia Police Academy diplomas he certainly didn't want to make it appear as though he didn't appreciate their professional presence, but just having them standing around and watching was spooky. Finally, Lieutenant Potocnak suggested that if they wanted to be involved, they should call up and get the FBI crime lab guys down to go over the trucks. The FBI men discussed that, and decided against it.

"It's not really our jurisdiction yet," one of them told the lieutenant.

"Look," Potocnak told them, "if you're not going to do anything, then get the hell out of our way."

So they left. Pat liked that. Jimmy was the kind of guy who took shit from nobody.

When the feds left, Pat got back to work. He interviewed the other witnesses gathered in the Purolator Building and then took a walk up Swanson Street. The company had gotten the names of the two men Proctor and Saracino had encountered on the street by the empty tub. One was Thomas Piacentino, who had been working at his father's junkyard near where the tubs had fallen. He related the whole sequence to Pat:

The yellow tub falls. In the minute or two that follow, one or two cars come down Swanson, ease around the obstacle, and drive on. Then one stops suddenly, and a man laughs loud enough for Piacentino to hear forty yards away, pulls two white things—they look like gunnysacks—out of the container, throws one into the front seat of the car, gets in, then jumps back out to throw the second bag into the backseat. The car then takes off fast around the corner. Piacentino and his brother Charles walk out to have a look at the container, and just as they reach it the armored truck comes barreling back up Swanson and out jumps this guard, who looks real nervous.

"What did the car look like?" Pat asked.

"A maroon Chevy Malibu with the right front fender painted blue," said Piacentino. This guy was terrific.

"What about the guy who grabbed the bags?"

"He looked to be in his late twenties, early thirties," said Piacentino. "He had thinnish hair, blond or light brown."

This all supported the drivers' version. When Pat got back to the company property he briefed Potocnak, and the lieutenant asked the company executives to lock him in the armored car. It seemed like a strange request. One of the first things the execs had done was demonstrate the elaborate locking mechanism on the trucks, to demonstrate how impossible Proctor's and Saracino's story was. There were two doors in back. The left door had to be closed and fastened with a padlock before the right door could be closed, so that one was usually kept shut. The right door fastened high and low with

two steel rods that fitted into slots. The rods were maneu-
vered back and forth by rotating the door handle first to the
right and then to the left. Once closed, a button at the center
of the handle was pushed to lock it in place.

"Humor me," said the lieutenant.

So they closed him in back and then carefully closed and
locked both doors.

Potocnak then leaned back and gave the doors a strong
kick with the sole of his foot. The right door gave a loud snap
and popped open.

It was dark when Pat left the Purolator property that
evening. He and the other detectives knew the drivers had told
the truth. Piacentino's story had convinced Pat. It didn't sound
like a lie. Too many fine details. It had meshed with the drivers' story perfectly. Jimmy's door demonstration, which had em-
barrassed the hell out of the Puralator executives, had clinched
it. That had been fun to watch. But if the drivers were telling
the truth, if the money had fallen off the truck, then this case
had just gone from routine to very hard. Pat mulled over what
he knew as he twice retraced the route taken by the armored
car from the Federal Reserve Bank to Swanson Street. If somebody had just driven by and picked the money up, and that
appeared to be what had happened, how were you going to find
him if he was intent on keeping it? Purolator was ready to put
up a $50,000 reward. But it takes a special breed of honesty to
willingly trade $1.2 million for $50,000.

The detective thought about what a smart man would do
if he wanted to keep a find like this. First he'd stuff it in his

closet and tell no one. That was key. *Tell no one.* The second
most important thing would be patience. If you waited a few
months, people would stop looking. You could start gradually
spending the money then, take a trip someplace nice, open a
few bank accounts in scattered locations. You wouldn't want
to deposit more than a few thousand at a time in any one account, but how much trouble could it be to open a new bank
account every day? Most people spent their days earning money;
you could spend yours figuring out what to do with what
you had. There were worse jobs. Gradually you could transfer
money around, consolidate it. If you went about it that way,
no one would ever catch you.

Philadelphia was a city of six million people. The *only* way
to make a mistake would be to start talking about it and passing out hundreds right away. Nobody was that dumb, but Pat
knew that was his only chance.

Then again, Swanson Street was no main thoroughfare.
It was a neighborhood shortcut. The only people who used it
were those who worked along that stretch of waterfront . . . and
those who lived nearby. He was looking for a young man with
thin blond or light brown hair.

And there was that maroon Chevy Malibu with a dinged
right front fender.

4

You have to work at believing a stroke of luck like this. Joey and the boys felt an immediate need to hold the cellophane bundles in their hands, tear off the packaging, and feel and smell the bills. John Behlau turned south on Front Street and stopped his father's car in front of the Coyle house. Joey took the bigger of the two canvas bags and sprinted up four front stairs. Jed carried the other bag. He and John followed Joey inside.

They ran upstairs to Joe's room, tore open the second money bag, and dumped the contents on his bed. The three stood gaping at the treasure. There was bundle after compressed cellophane bundle of cash, more than a hundred of them, more money than they had ever seen. Each bundle was wrapped with a paper band that read $10,000! All the bills appeared to be hundreds.

Joey was delirious with joy. He shouted, he leapt, he laughed. He kept embracing and kissing John and Jed, who didn't mind. Joey kept saying it was like a scene in a movie, like a scene in a movie. He felt more excitement than he knew how to express. Every time he looked down at the pile of bundles on his bed it was almost like he expected it not to be there.

Of course, somebody was going to be looking for this money. After the initial excitement, reality began to intrude. Joey, John, and Jed stood around the big Colonial-style bed and excitedly discussed their find. They figured the money belonged to the government, that it had fallen off one of the Purolator armored cars that rolled on and off the company lot at all hours of the day and night. The cops were going to hear of anyone flashing hundred-dollar bills. John and Jed wondered what kind of a reward there might be. But if Joey had even one fleeting thought of returning this bounty it was banished before it was fully formed. Finders keepers, man.

"It's mine," Joey told the boys. "I worked hard all my life. My hands are all busted up. I got nothin'."

He was no fancy talker so he had no words to express it, but Joey felt at that moment like he had been touched by destiny, by the hand of God. His father had smiled down from heaven on his troubles. *This was his chance.* He had never felt more sure of a thing in his life. It was perfect! He had done nothing wrong. No crime had been committed. He hadn't hurt anyone. It was money from heaven. It was money meant for him. Finders keepers—if he could just figure out how not to blow it.

Joey breathed deeply and tried to calm himself. He had to think clearly now.

"You can't tell anybody," Joey told them.

"Not even my dad?" asked Jed.

"No," said Joey. Nobody. Not even their parents or girl-friends. John and Jed were surprised at how serious Joey had suddenly become, how he moved to take control of the situation.

"I'll take care of everything," he said. "I don't want to hear anymore talk about reward money. This money is mine—*ours,*" he corrected himself. If it worked out, they would get a share of the money, too, he said. If it didn't, it was on him.

"Leave it to me," he said.

Joey may have looked like he was in control, but inside he was reeling. The problem seemed overwhelming. He would have to find a way of breaking the hundreds into smaller bills. But how? Where? Joey knew he needed help. And the man who first came to mind was his friend Carl Masi.

5

Carl Masi had been a fighter once. After World War II he had boxed as a lightweight for a few years before settling back in Philadelphia as a typesetter. At fifty-four he was still a muscular man with square features and curly gray hair. But Masi's heart was failing. Surgeons had opened his chest twice from neck to belly to make repairs. The doctors were always cheerful and optimistic but Masi didn't expect to live much longer. This had softened his manner, which was quiet anyway. It seemed there was no surprise or anger or fear that could overcome his will to savor what life he had left. His two daughters were grown; the older one was married. His wife, Dee, worked at Fidelity Bank. Since he couldn't hold a regular job anymore, Masi worked some nights as a bouncer for the Purgatory Club on Second Street, which was owned by a friend, even though in his condition he could hardly be expected to mix it up with anyone.

Masi knew Joey Coyle and his family from the neighborhood. Over the years he had taken a special liking to Joey. The kid had no father and he had no son. Joey was trouble sometimes, he took drugs and drank too much and gave his poor mother fits, but Masi saw that he was a good-hearted kid. Carl got mad when he saw other men taking advantage of Joey. They knew he made good money on the docks and they knew he had poor judgment. He was easily misled. Send the kid out with a roll of cash in his pockets and he would come home high, happy, bruised, and broke. But Masi was indulgent. He was past the point of being riled by failed expectations, his own or anyone else's. He never gave up on Joey. He had gotten the kid a job as a doorman for the Purgatory Club. And it was there that Joey observed that Masi knew personally some of the shadowy, serious men who were part of the Philadelphia/Atlantic City mob.

Once Carl Masi's name popped into Joey's head he clung to it like a lifeline. Leaving Jed with the money, he and John got back in the Chevy and drove to a Sunoco station on Oregon Avenue. From a pay phone he called Masi's house. Masi's daughter answered.

"This is Joey. It's important."

"He's not home," she said. "You can call Mom at work."

So Joe dialed Dee Masi at the bank.

"Where's your old man?" he asked.

"He should be picking me up soon," she said. "What's wrong?"

"You comin' home now?"

"Yes."

"Good. I'll see you there," said Joey, and then teased her a little. "Got somethin' to show you."

John drove Joey first to another dealer's house, where he at last copped some speed. As he rode back to his house, Joey impatiently fingered the plastic bag full of white powder in his jacket pocket.

At home, he prepared to inject himself in the kitchen. The ritual was a familiar one. Pour some powder on a spoon, add a few drops of water, hold the spoon over a flame until the powder was mixed well with the water, draw the white liquid up into a hypodermic needle, pick a vein in his right forearm—they were getting harder to find—and inject. Joey's need had grown so urgent that when he had the drug he performed this ritual almost every hour.

Fired up again, Joey returned to his bedroom and the treasure. He sat for a long time just staring at it, feeling his heart race as the drug kicked into full gear. Then he dragged two Bishop Newman schoolbags, small square suitcases of stiff black cardboard, from his closet. He stacked the bundles in them neatly, then folded the canvas bags in on top of them. Then he and John took the suitcases to the car and drove to Masi's row house on South 29th Street.

"He's *connected*," Joey explained. John took this to mean that Masi had ties to the mob. "Carl will know what to do with it," Joey said.

Masi's daughter let them in. They took the suitcases to a front bedroom on the second floor. It was the biggest bedroom in the house, second-floor front, with beige walls and standard sixties-style department-store furnishings. White curtains over the front windows allowed only a dim glow of light into the room. Joe set the black cases on the bed.

He removed the money in fistfuls. Each of the $10,000 bands was marked with a set of three initials, for each of the tellers who had counted it. Joey marveled at the rituals of procedure revealed by the money's packaging. The initials were repeated on each bundle in the same order, on the top $100 bill, and then again on the tag at the top of the canvas bag. He began to remove the wrappers and tags. After he had accumulated a mound of cellophane and paper wrappers, he stuffed that and the lead seals from the tops of the torn canvas bags into a doubled paper grocery bag. He got a can of lighter fluid from Masi's daughter and took it out to the tiny patio behind the house. He stuffed the bag inside a trash can, soaked it with lighter fluid, and set it on fire. Joey stood by until it smoldered and then squirted more fluid on it. He kept the inside of the can burning until all the paper was gone and the seals were molten discs of lead. When the lead cooled he took the dull smooth discs from the bottom of the can and dropped them in his pocket. He didn't want to leave a trace.

While Joe was doing these things, John left to retrieve Jed. Back up in the bedroom Joe piled the wrapped and unwrapped hundreds into neat stacks of $50,000, and then set them in a bureau drawer. Then he went down to the kitchen to wait for Dee and Carl. John and Jed returned and flopped on the plastic-covered furniture in the Masis' living room.

Carl and Dee arrived at about four o'clock. Joey met them at the door.

"Come on upstairs," he said. "I got somethin' for ya."

It looked to Masi like Joey was all cranked up again. The older man eyed suspiciously the two strange boys in his living room. Joey told John and Jed to wait for them downstairs. Then he and the Masis walked upstairs together. In the bedroom Joey pulled open the drawer. Carl and Dee Masi stared at the money silently.

"Joey, did you kill anybody?" Masi asked.

"No!" Joe laughed.

"Did you hurt anybody?"

"No!"

Joey was impatient with his friend's subdued response. He drew the cash from the drawer and made a pile of it on the bed. Then he picked up Dee and dropped her on top of it. Dee laughed. Masi just looked on quietly. He didn't know where the money came from, but he knew it couldn't legitimately belong to Joey Coyle. Then he remembered. On the radio in the car he had heard that more than a million dollars had fallen off the back of an armored truck.

"I heard about this," he said. "This is the money that fell off the truck, ain't it?"

"Yeah," said Joey.

"Joey, you ought to get in touch with a lawyer and get in touch with Purolator and see what they'll give you for a reward."

"No way, Carl. It's mine. I found it."

"Joey, they're not going to let you keep it."

"How they gonna know?"

Masi knew Joey and he knew there was no way he and these two kids downstairs were going to keep a secret like that. They were too excited, too young, too careless. He knew what Joey was like when he was all cranked up. It was going to be all over South Philly in a couple of days, no avoiding it.

"They already got a description of your car," Masi said. "I heard it on the radio coming over. Maroon Chevy with a blue front fender. There it is parked right outside. You're crazy."

Joey felt a touch of panic. It hadn't occurred to him that somebody might have seen them picking up the money.

"I come to you for help," Joey said. Joey explained that he had called Masi because he was *connected*. He wanted somebody from the mob to help him change the money into smaller bills. He would be willing to share it, he said.

"Could you get in touch with a few people? Get the money broke down from hundreds?"

Whatever they were going to do, first they would have to get rid of the car. It sat out in front like a red flag. It was already half past four. The local evening news would be on at six. Then everybody in Philadelphia would be looking for a maroon Chevy with blue primer on the front fender.

Joey and Carl went downstairs and explained to John that they had to ditch his father's car. John was horrified.

"It's my dad's!" he told them. "What am I going to tell him? What are you going to do with it?"

"Look, we're just going to take the car over the bridge and sit it over in Jersey for the time being," said Joey. "If we don't ditch it, it's going to give us away."

John reluctantly went out to the car, removed some of his own things and some scraps of ID from the glove compartment, and handed over the keys. Joey drove the Chevy and Masi followed in his own car. Joey held his breath as they crossed the Walt Whitman Bridge. His gaze swept from one rearview mirror to the other. He expected to get pulled over at any minute. He drove to the 200 block of Mercer Street in Gloucester, near the shipyard where his older brother, Billy, was a supervisor, and parked it. Then he and Masi drove to a bar for a few drinks. They arrived at the bar in time for the nightly news. That's when the magnitude of what had happened really sank in. The missing money was the lead story. The reporters showed pictures of the Purolator truck and the company lot, and there was a company executive interviewed. He looked nervous. Joey watched and felt powerful and proud, maybe for the first time in his life. He was the guy! He had the money! He was proud of himself for ditching that Malibu. That had been smart. Many men believe they are capable of functioning coolly in a crisis, but how many of them actually meet the test when it comes?

John and Jed were waiting with Dee and her daughter when they returned two hours later. They had watched the nightly newscast, too, and it had kicked up something akin to stage fright in the boys' bellies.

In Joey's absence they had begun to get cold feet.

"What did you do with my father's car?" John asked.

"Don't worry," said Masi.

"We should get it crushed down," said Joey.

John freaked.

"That's my father's car!"

"Okay, okay. Jesus!" said Joey. "We'll buy him a new car. We'll buy him three new cars! Tell him you're having it re-painted. You'll get it back in a couple of days."

The six of them sat in the Masis' small living room before the TV and discussed what they had learned on the news. They had been a little surprised at how much attention the story was getting. Everyone told Joe that maybe he ought to consider giving the money back.

"Don't worry about it, don't worry about it," said Joey, his gruff voice rising with impatience. "There's been no crime committed. If there's anything that goes down, it's their fault not ours! Like, they're negligent for losin' the money. Nobody has said there's a reward or anything. We just gotta lay low. We're rich. They know it's gone, but they don't know we got it."

6

What happened next that evening is a part of the story that retreats into shadow. One of the abiding certainties of life in South Philly was the mob, a long-standing, hierarchical, *neighborhood* crime organization. There were those who would smile and shake their heads and swear that such a thing didn't exist. But several times a year an otherwise healthy man in South Philly was found on the sidewalk or in the trunk of a car with a belly full of pasta and a bullet hole in his head. Decent, patriotic folks who went to church every Sunday and washed their children's mouths out with soap for swearing would shrug their shoulders and turn their heads and fail with alacrity to summon any outrage over this. The shadow world of violence coexisted with virtue in South Philly, just as in the heart of even the best of men there was sin. It was not spoken of. Even those who would speak of it were silenced by fear. There were things said or seen that become secrets vaulted so securely that the truth stayed locked beyond the reach of any serum, courtroom, or oath.

That night at Carl Masi's house came a man from these shadows. He was called Sonny. He was a man in his mid-fifties, short and thick, with glasses and a balding forehead. He spoke with a deep, gruff voice. Joey knew he was Mario "Sonny" Riccobene, younger brother of the bearded, hunchbacked Harry Riccobene. The two were among the most notorious organized-crime leaders in Philadelphia. Joe felt a chill of fear and pleasure to be with him in the same room. He and Masi and Sonny went upstairs where the money was still in a big pile on the bed. The others waited downstairs.

"What's the matter? You got a problem?" asked Sonny.

Joey showed him cash. He explained that it was the Purolator money. The money that had fallen off the truck, one-million-two.

"You gonna give it back?"

"I figure there wasn't, like, no c-c-crime committed," said Joey. He had a tendency to stutter when he was too excited.

"Is there a reward?"

"Like, the money is being looked for—it was on radio and TV and all—but they ain't put up no reward," said Joey. "So, I figure, these people lose one-point-two million and they ain't puttin' up no reward for it! And I got these stacks of money, and its very real, and they're offerin', over there, like nothing, a row of zeroes, you know what I mean? Hey, it ain't greed, but show me something to show good faith."

"What are you gonna do with it?" asked Sonny.

Joey had given this some thought. He spelled out his plan.

"Look, I think it would be smart to take this money and split it in three directions. Four for you, four for me, four for Carl. Put it in three different places, right? That way, if they catch me, I still got eight hundred thousand dollars when I get out. And you take the four for you and you give me back three in small bills. The other one hundred thousand is for you. Whatever. You know what I'm sayin'? Like, just get me back the three hundred thousand in small bills as quick as you can and you can keep a hundred thousand just for doin' it."

Sonny nodded. Joe stood alone in the bedroom while the two older men conferred in the dark hallway. Then they returned.

"I think I could do that," said Sonny. "We could take it to the casinos and play it. You win some and you lose some, but that way you pass as much of it as you can as fast as you can. We could do that. These aren't consecutive bills. It would take me a day or two."

Joey was delighted. It was more than merely getting the help he sought. It was a kind of recognition. They had bought his plan! Joe felt . . . well, *honored*. He sorted the money into three roughly equal piles. He put his cut back in one of the black cases. Masi and Sonny put theirs in brown paper bags. Then they came back downstairs. Before leaving the house, Sonny turned to John and Jed. Silently, he put his forefinger to his lips and then, pointing toward them, held up his thumb like the hammer of a gun and let it fall. Both boys got the message.

Carl Masi would live much longer than he'd expected, but even in later years when he was asked to tell the story of Joey Coyle and the money that fell off the truck, long after the case was over and the police had lost interest in it, he would leave out the part about another man coming into his house that night.

"Wasn't there a man who visited that night?" I asked him once, after the story was well known.

"Here?"

"Yes. Others who were here have said that Sonny Riccobene came over that night."

"No way. Sonny Riccobene has never set foot in my house."

"No? Did anyone else come in?"

"Joey brought somebody in here, but it wasn't Sonny Riccobene. Those kids are crazy. I know Sonny Riccobene. Those kids are wrong. I bet you if you showed those boys Sonny Riccobene face to face they wouldn't even know him."

"Do you know who it was who came over that night?"

"Some guy. But it wasn't Sonny Riccobene. I wish those kids were here looking at me when they said that. Because they're wrong. They always said that it was Sonny Riccobene. They had the name 'Sonny.' And they said it was Sonny Riccobene. But they're full of shit. They are one hundred percent wrong. Do you think a guy like Sonny Riccobene would have let somebody like Joey Coyle keep two-thirds of that kind of money? They're crazy, spreading stories like that. Sonny Riccobene has never been in this house. That's the truth."

7

With his plan in motion, Joey felt like a man who had wrestled a giant to the earth, and even though he knew the match was not over, he could take a deep breath again for the first time since finding the money that afternoon. Soon after Sonny left, Masi drove Joey, John, and Jed back to Front Street. They left the remaining $800,000 in the bureau drawer in Masi's bedroom. Joey and the boys felt unburdened.

Masi arranged for a friend to loan Joe a big boat of a car, a car equal to his prosperous mood. It was an emerald-green Cadillac El Dorado with a white convertible top and a white interior. It was . . . well, *perfect*.

Waiting for Joey at home was his girlfriend, a tiny, thin blond woman named Linda Rutter. Linda was just eighteen, and she was seeing Joey somewhat on the sly. She had another boyfriend, a more respectable boyfriend, from whom she kept Joey secret. This had been going on for about a year. At the house on the floor under the mail slot Linda had found Joey's seven-hundred-dollar check. She had taken it right away to a check-cashing place in the neighborhood where they knew her and Joey, and they had cashed it for her. She knew Joey was hungry for that money, and she was looking forward to blowing some of it that night. But when Joey came in he looked strung out. Without hesitation, he told her what had happened.

"I'm the guy!" he said.

"What guy?"

"The guy who found the money!"

"What money?" Linda asked, but then, looking at Joey's grin, it dawned on her.

"The Purolator money?"

They both jumped up and down with excitement. Joey then fixed injections for Linda and for himself, and they wound up in bed, screwing in a wild state of excitement.

Later that evening, they went out to buy groceries at the Pathmark supermarket on Oregon Avenue. When they returned home with armfuls of bags, John and Jed were waiting.

Joey was in no mood to get into it with the boys again. He knew that Sonny had scared them badly enough that they weren't going to tell anyone about the money. So he told them that he didn't want to talk in front of his girlfriend and that he would meet them in half an hour on the corner. John and Jed left. They waited down the street, and then watched angrily as Joey and Linda left the house, got back in the Cadillac, and drove off.

Joey drove to his sister Ellen's house a few blocks away. Ellen was ironing. She was a big, blond, smart, outgoing woman six years Joey's senior who tried to mother him the way she did her own children. She saw her baby brother as a vulnerable, artistic boy who lacked something she couldn't quite define, maybe maturity or self-confidence, to manage life on his own. It wasn't just that Joey screwed up a lot; he refused to take advantage of the skills and opportunities he had. It was almost as though he was afraid to try, afraid to accomplish anything, because any success would bring with it responsibility, and Joey knew he couldn't handle it. Like the time Joe had worked out a mechanical device to keep drivers down on the docks from accidently blowing out transmissions on the lifts. It was cunningly clever and original, everybody agreed. Ellen had forced Joe to sit down and sketch the thing and sent him to a lawyer to see about getting a patent so he could get some profit out of it. Joe had drawn it up and then gone to see the lawyer, but when the lawyer called and left messages, Joey never called back. You could drive yourself crazy trying to figure out why he was that way and get no closer to the truth. It was just the way he was. People loved Joey, but the same boyish qualities that made him lovable also made him impossible. Ellen, on the other hand, was a rock. She was as motivated and dependable as Joey was not. Ellen had been especially worried about him since their mother was bedridden and had to leave the old house to move in with her. She knew he was using drugs heavily and that he wasn't working. She worried about him. When she looked at his battered body she saw a little blond-haired boy in a white suit on the day of his First Communion. She prayed for him. But there was only so much she could do.

Leaving Linda in the car outside, Joey went upstairs to see his mom, who was watching television with Ellen's eight-year-old daughter, Katie. His mother was sitting up in bed. She looked bad. Katie was on the floor by the TV. Joe spent about fifteen minutes with them, talking quietly. He offered to let his niece in on a big secret. He made her swear not to tell, and the little girl opened her eyes wide and swore it. Then he told her that he had come into a lot of money and that they were all going to be rich.

"You're my baby, don't worry about nothin'," he told her. "I'm going to be leaving for a little while, but I'll be sending for everybody. We're going to fly Mama out of the city, get her to some really good doctors."

When Joey came back downstairs, Ellen thought he looked upset. She wanted to talk to him so she offered him a cup of coffee.

"No, thanks," he said. "I got to go." He was moving around the room, looking out the windows and down the street.

"What's wrong, Joey?" Ellen asked.

"Nothing, nothing. Everything is all right."

He said good-bye and walked out the door.

DAY TWO

Friday
February 27, 1981

1

And who hasn't dreamed of finding or winning or inheriting a million dollars?

It might be argued that the Purolator Armored Car Co.'s misfortune was hardly as important to the lives and well-being of Philadelphia citizens as, say, President Reagan's visit to the British prime minister to discuss international trade, or the mounting number of murdered children in Atlanta, victims of a serial killer, or the congressional debate over sending military aid to embattled Central American governments, but in white honor boxes on sunny street corners and folded on the front steps of hundreds of thousands of homes that Friday came the morning paper with this story stripped across the top: $1.2 MILLION FALLS OFF TRUCK 2 FLEE WITH IT.

As the city rose to sunny, warmer skies and the promise of a springlike weekend in late winter, and as breakfast was prepared in millions of busy kitchens, readers skimmed reports of the world's weightier matters but read to the last line the story of the million dollars that fell off the truck and then wondered aloud along Broad Street and Market Street and on subways and trains and buses about what *they* would do.

A columnist for the Philadelphia *Daily News* had it all planned.

"I've been doing some fantasizing of my own about finding $1.2 million . . . ," wrote Greg Walter. "Who among us hasn't? Had such a serendipitous event occurred, I've day-dreamed, I would have quickly stashed most of the dough and headed for the first plane stopping at Key West, Florida. By the time the alarm had been sounded, I would have been in the sea green land of the hundred dollar bill and the cocaine cowboy. A recent trip to this southeasternmost part of the United States has convinced me that there are more hundreds floating around down there than are stashed in all the Purolator vaults in the country."

Another citizen asked that his name not be used but suggested he would have hidden the bulk of the money and gone immediately on a long trip, maxing out his credit cards and savings to sustain his travels, to return a year or more later to recover the treasure once the trail had cooled.

Elizabeth Delaney of South Philly said she would most definitely return the money herself, but that her friends had discussed going on expensive trips, paying off their bills, and gambling heavily in Atlantic City.

Steven Farmer, a butcher with evident cosmopolitan experience, told a reporter that the reward money wasn't enough:

"Over in Europe, they give you twenty percent if you return money. If I found the money, I would be too scared to use it, afraid of being caught. I have a friend who works for the

Federal Reserve Bank and he told me they have the serial number of that money because they got the numbers on anything that leaves there, especially the large amounts."

Of course, the right thing to do would be to give it back. There was no question about that. The news stories helped this ethical certainty along by pointing out that in the state of Pennsylvania it was a crime to keep something valued at more than $250 without making any effort to find its rightful owner. Still, in a corner of every mind that considered the matter, there was the enticing idea of keeping it. People asked each other, What would *you* do?

There was another story that day of particular interest to South Philly. Police had found the body of one Frank Stillitano, thirty, in a parking garage at Philadelphia International Airport. Stillitano, who was wanted at the time for questioning in another mob murder, had been shot once in the leg and once behind the left ear, packed in the trunk of a car, and parked in an airport lot for the long, long term. It was the latest in a series of mob killings—there would be a dozen in 1981—sparked by the 1980 assassination of longtime Philadelphia mafia boss Angelo Bruno. News of the new murder had already made its way around the neighborhood without benefit of modern media.

In the same newspapers, Lieutenant Jimmy Potocnak, head of the twelve-man unit at South Detective Division assigned to the case, was departing from usual departmental practice to chat about the ongoing investigation with reporters. He was desperate.

"I think the person or persons who have this money are too scared to turn it in," he said. "But we will make no arrest if they turn in the money."

The lieutenant made sure that the reporter jotted down his phone numbers, MU-6-7640 and MU-6-3013. He wanted those numbers right there in the newspapers. He was asking for help.

2

Joey Coyle and his girl, Linda Rutter, hadn't seen the newspaper. It was early morning on the blue Ben Franklin Bridge. Joey steered the El Dorado around Alexander Calder's bright stainless-steel approximation of old Ben's kite and key, and headed into the morning rush hour. His million-dollar find was all over the morning airwaves. Linda kept punching the radio buttons. Joey wasn't really listening. He was so pumped up he was shaking. He had scored more speed the night before and had been injecting himself at intervals. It was all he could do to sit still behind the wheel of the car. He and Linda had spent most of the night celebrating at a series of Jersey watering holes and at the Admiral Wilson Motel, where they registered as Mr. and Mrs. Joseph Coyle. But Joey hadn't been able to stay there for long. All through Thursday night they had moved from the motel room to bar to bar to bar and then back to the motel room. The combination of their excitement over the money and the rush of the drug swept them along in such an exhilarating tear that all they could do was keep moving. Sex, drugs, alcohol, and motion . . . Joey couldn't get enough. He had no desire to eat or sleep. They had checked out of the motel that morning because Joey decided he had to show Linda the money.

Truth is, a worm of doubt had crept into Joey's jubilation. He began to worry that his friend Carl Masi and the mobster might not be content to just baby-sit his million.

Joey's fears grew when he and Linda arrived at Masi's to find the two men huddled together in the kitchen. Sonny stood when they entered, and then abruptly left.

"We want to take another look," said Joey.

Masi took the couple upstairs to the bedroom. He showed Joey the black case filled with his third of the money. The other two suitcases were gone. Joey asked Linda to unwrap more of the bundles and stack the bills on the bureau while he talked with Masi in the hall.

"Where the fuck is the rest of it?" Joey asked.

The older man explained he had hidden his third, and that Sonny was leaving for Las Vegas that morning with the other third. Masi could see how spooked Joey was.

"Stop worrying," he told him. Masi reminded Joey that the plan to split up the find had been his own. It took time to move that much money. He and Sonny had run into a few snags, but it was all going to be okay.

Joey trusted his friend but the worry was hard to shake. The feeling had just started coming over him early that morning and it was getting stronger. The speed seemed to amplify it.

"I'm going to take my third with me," he said.

So when Masi left to drive Dee to work at the bank, Joey and Linda stuffed the remaining cash and loose wrappers into the black case and pointed the El Dorado back home.

3

U pstairs in his bedroom, Joey finished unwrapping the cash. He arranged the hundred-dollar bills into forty stacks, one hundred to a pile, and fastened each bundle with a rubber band. He gave Linda a coffee can and told her to take the cellophane and paper wrappers to the bathroom, burn them, and flush the ashes down the toilet.

Then Joey drove Linda over to her sister's house on Roseberry Street. He planned to spend the day alone at home, laying low. He told Linda he would return for her that night.

Back home on Front Street, Joe again injected himself with speed. He sprinkled the white powder on a spoon, mixed it with drops of water, warmed it over a flame, drew up the mixture into a syringe, and slipped the needle into a vein in his right forearm. Over the years the drug had ceased to give him anything that could be called pleasure. Addiction was like riding a devilish engine that worked double, triple time. At first it had been fun and made Joey feel all-powerful, vibrantly sexual, and so much happier than he normally felt. But then, as the drug's grip on him hardened, he began to feel as though he were stuck on a wild ride. Even when his mind and body grew tired it stayed strapped to the same frantic engine, which ran on and on at its double, triple speed through day and night, dulling both pleasure and pain. He felt pinioned to it like some pathetic, wildly gesticulating marionette. And it was then that the drug played its meanest trick. Instead of giving Joey a rush of energy and potency, he found he now needed the regular injections to calm himself down. After only a few hours without a boost, the engine threatened to careen out of control, his senses reeling, his mind muddled and tormented by imagined terrors, his limbs shaking and in pain. In time, the only thing that hurt more than staying on the engine was getting off.

This time with the sudden surge of relief came another, stronger surge of fear. Staring at all the green bundles, Joey felt suddenly overwhelmed by the challenge of hanging onto it. The idea of finding that much money was proving to be more thrilling than the actual experience, much as the highs he got by shooting speed had long ago stopped living up to his expectations. The hard truth about life, which most people learned but that Joey had not, was that things had to be earned to be fully enjoyed. Success, accomplishment, the admiration of the world—these were all things that could not be faked, or purchased with a needle or a windfall. When Joey first found the money, it promised instant wealth, status, and happiness. With it he would possess everything, just like when the drug worked, and he felt for a time like he owned the whole world. Instead, the money seemed to own him, just as the drugs owned him. How could he keep it? Where should he hide it? How would he spend it? What were the right moves?

He expected the door to break down and the police to stomp in at any moment. Maybe he should have just left the cash with Masi. He got up and checked out the windows, just to make sure. Down the street in one direction he saw John and Jed out working on a pickup truck. In the other direction was a police car. It cruised slowly down the block, past Joey's house, and turned right on Wolf Street at the end of the block. The neighborhood was crawling with cop cars.

Joey paced and fidgeted inside his house. He had to find a safe place for the $400,000. But where? He gathered the bundles into a brown paper bag and took it down to the kitchen. Underneath the kitchen floor he had long ago built a safe spot to hide his drugs. Twice the police had searched his house looking for drugs, and both times they had missed the hiding place. Joey slid the bag of cash into the open space under the floor and covered it. At last, he could relax.

But only for a minute. Because right away the worry came back. Just because it had been a good hiding place for drugs, that didn't make it a good enough spot for four hundred thousand. The cops would be looking a lot harder for the money than the drugs. A hiding place under the floor? No. They probably had dogs or something that could sniff out cash. Joey could almost smell the dogs in the house. He checked all the windows again. Then he returned to the kitchen, uncovered the hiding place, and removed the bag of money.

There had to be a better place. He walked down the steps to the basement, looking for the perfect spot. He poked around down there for about ten minutes, stumped, when he hit upon the idea of hiding the money inside his hot water heater. He set down the bag and fetched his tools. After disconnecting the piping, Joey removed the top of the heater and pulled out the fiberglass insulation from its outer and inner walls. Then he stuffed the money into the space, replaced the fiberglass around the upper rim, and reconnected all the fittings. He worked up a sweat doing it. The whole job took about half an hour. Unburdened at last, Joey went upstairs to the kitchen and made a cup of instant coffee.

Still the wheels kept turning. The hot water heater was gas. It had a pilot light inside of it. What if the money got too hot and caught on fire? It would all burn up! Leaving the coffee cup full on the kitchen table, Joey bolted for his tools and returned with them to the basement. Working methodically now, he disassembled the piping on top of the heater again, removed the fiberglass from the upper rim, and then pulled all the money bundles back out. Then he put the heater back together.

Two hours had elapsed and the money was still in the black cardboard suitcase at his feet. With his tools in one hand and the money bag in the other, Joey walked upstairs to the second-floor bathroom. He had another idea. Getting down on all fours, he went to work on the toilet. He unbolted it from the floor, working with his plumbing tools, and shut off the water connection. It felt good to be working with his hands; it calmed him. With the toilet bowl disconnected, he tilted it up. Underneath, under and around the porcelain underbelly of the bowl, was a large enough empty space for him to stash the bundles of cash. This, he thought, was perfect. Joey had known dealers who hid drugs there because the smell of the toilet bowl masked the odor of the stash from police dogs. With the underside of the bowl fully stuffed, he reconnected the pipes and bolted the toilet back to the floor.

Finally! He now felt relaxed enough to shower and change clothes. He made himself another cup of coffee and sat uneasily in the living room. Joey found laying low extremely difficult. Every few minutes he got up to check the windows, pulling back his mother's old curtains and peering out. He watched up and down the street. He paced. When the effects of the speed began to ease he would fix himself again. Taking a trip upstairs to urinate, Joey found himself no longer comfortable with the money inside the toilet bowl. It just didn't *feel* right to him. He couldn't explain it, even to himself, but he went straight for his tools and began disassembling the toilet again.

Before he had finished putting things back together, Joey had thought of an even better hiding place. There was an empty space between the outside wall of the house and the plaster inside walls. From the closet in his mother's bedroom he could climb up into the space between the ceiling and the roof beams, a tight squeeze, crawl the twenty feet across to the front of the house, and then lower the bag into the opening between the two front walls. It was a delicate task. His mother's bedroom had a drop ceiling of tiles suspended on a fragile aluminum matrix. Joey carefully edged out along the wooden ceiling beams. He lowered the bag of money into the space behind the front wall. It fit like it belonged there.

Up in the small space between the drop ceiling and the underside of the roof, Joey realized that there was no way for him to turn around. He would have to crawl backward on the support beams to the open space where he could climb down. This was not easy. He edged backward slowly, stopped, caught his breath, and then edged out a little more. He was about half-way to the opening when, with a sudden terrific jolt, he abruptly found himself on the floor of his mother's bedroom. He was too cranked up to feel any pain. It took him a few seconds to figure out what had happened. He had momentarily blacked out. Around him on the floor were several bent pieces of aluminum stripping and two of the large tiles from the ceiling. Overhead was a gaping hole. Crawling backward, his knee had missed the two-by-four beam. Joe had been thrown suddenly off balance and his whole hundred-and-seventy-five-pound frame had crashed through the ceiling and plunged eight feet down to the floor, where he now sat looking up.

It took Joey about an hour to repair the drop ceiling. He bent the aluminum strips back into shape and refastened them, and then placed the tiles back. When he finished, Joe paused to inject himself with speed again, then decided that the money wasn't safe between the two walls. So he climbed back up into the crawl space, edged back over to the front of the house, and fished it out again.

4

Detective Pat Laurenzi had gone home to Roxborough in northwest Philadelphia late Thursday night. Before leaving the precinct station he had written reports of his work that day and sent out the following message to area police departments:

Wanted: theft, RSP, Consp. 2-26-81 appx. 2:30 P.M. on the hwy. Swanson and Wolf St. committed by 2 W/M's #I 20 to 30 yrs. light brown hair thin NFD #2 male were in a Maroon Chevy Malibu 1969 to 72. with a right front blue fender. males took from the Hwy. 2 canvas bags from a yellow container that fell from a Purolator Truck bags contained the amount of appx. $1.2 million dollars in cash in used $100 bills Ser# unknown, money was picked up from the Federal Reserve Bank at 6th Arch St. 2-26-81. Bags may have a tag white in color with the name Atlantic National Bank of Ventnor, N.J. Bags were tied by a rope-type tie and crimped with lead. for further info contact F.B.I. or South Detective Special Invest Unit Det. Laurenzi.

When he came back in to work at about eight the next morning, there was a stack of telephone tips. Calls had started dribbling in after the evening news Thursday night, and as public interest grew the tips accelerated. Every hundred-dollar bill in the region was suspect. People had seen the car in three states going in five different directions. One caller had seen the car in West Philadelphia by Drexel University, so Pat got in his car and spent a few hours cruising through that part of town. Nothing. Then he drove back to precinct to take more calls.

He obtained a search warrant for the junkyard, in case the brothers Piacentino had been less than forthcoming, but after driving over and surveying their fantastic expanse of debris, the detective realized that it would take weeks to conduct a proper search—there were simply too many places where the money could be hidden—and, besides, he tended to believe the brothers' story.

Back at the precinct, Pat knew he was stymied. There was nothing he could do but wait for something else to happen. At his gray metal desk, using a ruler as a straight edge, the detective drew a simple map of Swanson Street between Oregon and Wolf. He labeled in small squares the Purolator office and the junkyard, and drew a smaller square in the center right of the road and wrote next to it "Tub." He put other details in the drawing. A few yards up from the place where the tub had fallen there was a telephone pole, so he drew a small circle and next that wrote "Pole."

He scrutinized the drawing and it made him laugh. It was pitiful how little he had to go on.

He decided to just cruise the neighborhood, familiarizing himself with the layout of streets at that furthermost eastern edge of his beat. They had thrown a large number of uniformed units into these blocks, on foot, in cars, even a helicopter. They were looking for a Chevy Malibu with signs of body work on the front end, but short of that anything in the ballpark. He figured the brothers Piacentino might have been mistaken about the make or even the color. But so far the search had turned up nothing.

Waiting for something else to happen had stretched the day to frustrating lengths for the detective. But Pat was not disheartened. Despite all the crazy telephone tips, he felt sure that whoever had picked up the money bags lived right here in this network of narrow streets. And if that was true then the secret was bound to come out. This was South Philly. Nobody in these row-house blocks was going to find more than a million dollars without confiding the discovery to *someone*. And once that someone knew, somebody else would get the news, then someone else, and so on. It was human nature, an immutable law. Pat knew he had only to stick around and be ready.

He drove slowly, in widening circles, until he was about ten blocks away from Wolf and Swanson Streets, then he reversed direction and worked his way gradually back, making smaller and smaller circles. Then he started over again.

5

Joey left the house carrying the money in his squat black cardboard schoolbag. It was sunset. Over the rooftops behind him the concrete side of I-95 shone white against a purple sky. Across the city the sky glowed orange and pink, but down on his street it was already night. Police units were everywhere. Joey felt like the bag he carried had neon dollar signs printed on the outside, like his guilt glowed in the dark. His pulse pounded in his ears. When a helicopter passed overhead, most likely a rush hour traffic spotter for a local radio station, he felt sure it had been a police chopper and that they were watching him. He wanted to run, but then a cop rounded the corner down the block with a big dog on the leash. It was all Joey could do to keep himself from breaking into a run. He walked slowly the rest of the block to the El Dorado. He threw the bag on the seat next to him and started to drive, slowly and carefully, over Wolf Street seven blocks west toward his friend Mike DiCriscio's house.

He made it a few blocks before stopping. He jumped out with the bag, popped the trunk, put the bag inside, closed the trunk, and returned to the driver's seat. Then he drove on.

Mike was six years older than Joey. He was a tall man with an olive-dark complexion, a thick mustache, and dark, curly hair. Mike was a good talker, a serious fellow with a quiet sense of humor. He made a living by buying old homes and renovating them for resale. Joey thought of Mike as someone with a knack for making money with money. He respected him. He had begun to doubt Masi, and had decided that it would have been better to have brought the money to Mike in the first place to ask for help. But maybe Mike could tell him what to do with this slice of his bonanza.

It was dark when Mike let Joey into his living room, looking strung out and displaying this wild, silly grin. Mike and his wife, Marion, invited him into the kitchen for a cup of coffee.

They sat and talked. Mike complained about how slow his houses were turning over. He said that they were scrounging to keep up with the mortgage payments, trying to keep things together.

"Don't worry about it," said Joey, feeling suddenly magnanimous. "I'll take care of you. I'll give you anything you want."

This brought smiles to Mike's and Marion's faces. How could he expect to help them?

"Did you hear about the Purolator truck that dropped the million dollars that somebody came by and picked up?" Joey asked.

"Yeah."

"It's me."

Mike didn't respond.

"It's *me*," Joey repeated in a huge conspiratorial whisper. "I found the money."

Mike had seen Joey Coyle all hopped up like this. He figured the drug had really run away with him this time. So Joey walked him out to the car and opened the trunk. Mike could scarcely believe his eyes. The pile of cash in the bag looked like it ought to contain a lot more than a third of the missing million.

Joey admitted that he was in over his head. He needed Mike's help. First, he said, they had to talk to this guy Carl Masi about the rest of the money. Joey explained about Masi and the mob, and how he now wanted just to get back the money he had given his older friend.

It had taken a full day, but the thought had at last crossed Joey's mind that Masi and this fellow Sonny might not have the purest of motives. The more Joey pondered it, the more he realized that the mob had little incentive to return $800,000 to him. Joey was beginning to worry about that. Maybe he had screwed up already. He wanted to talk to Masi again, and he wanted somebody solid like Mike to be there to back him up.

When he phoned from Mike's house, Masi's daughter answered. She said her father wasn't home but that the two young men who had been with Joey the night before were back.

As if he didn't have enough problems already, Joey knew he would have to deal with John and Jed. He had parked John's father's car over in Jersey by the side of the road. They were going to want that back. And John and Jed were either going to want some part of the money or they were going to want to turn it back in. They had been leaning toward turning the money back in the night before. Joey asked Masi's daughter to put John on the phone.

"Don't move out of the house," Joey told him. "I'll be right over."

Both the younger men were angry about the way Joey had given them the slip the night before. The truth is, John had already told his father about what happened. He hadn't felt like he had a choice. How else was he to explain the missing car? His dad had been furious about that. So John had fessed up. Their car fit the description that was all over the news. It was a mess. Jed also had confided the whole thing to his mother. The parents of both young men had been adamant. They wanted them to retrieve the Behlaus' car and give back the money promptly, before matters got worse!

Joey stashed the black bag in the front closet of Mike's house, and the two of them drove the few blocks over to the Masis. When they arrived, John lit into Joey about his father's car. He didn't tell him that both he and Jed had already given up the secret to their parents. Instead he said that he and Jed had both decided on their own to return the money. It was too hot. They were scared. They wanted to end the whole adventure and collect the reward.

Joey was flabbergasted by the change in John's and Jed's attitude. He couldn't believe his ears. He exploded at them. How could they be so stupid!

"I worked hard years!" he said. "I worked eight-hour shifts all my life! I'm all scarred and banged up! I've worked too hard to have nothing! All my life!" Joey banged his hand down so hard on the Masis' living room table that his watch flew off his arm and skittered across the floor. "I can't get the money back now even if I want it!" he said. "The mafia has the money. There's no way we can get it back. They're *processing* it."

"Joe, there's a fifty-thousand-dollar reward," said Jed.

"From who?"

"From the Purolator Company."

"I ain't buyin' that," said Joey. "Look, who does this belong to? You don't know. It didn't say nothin' about Purolator on the bag. On the bag it said one thing, that's Federal Reserve, that's the United States. Now, if they put up a reward for it, fine, we'll talk about it, you know what I mean?"

But John and Jed persisted. The story was all over the city. The money belonged to Purolator. Everybody knew. There was a $50,000 reward for turning it in, which was more than what they had gotten out of it so far.

Joey scoffed at their new attitude.

"I am not giving the money back!" he said. "Fifty grand! A lousy fifty grand? We've got more than a million."

Joey told them he needed only a couple of days to make his getaway. He said he would leave the country, but he had to get the money broken down and make his arrangements first. He'd give the two of them their cut, and they could do whatever they wanted, but he wasn't going to give his back under any circumstances. He handed each of them a hundred-dollar bill, and warned them not to spend it until he was gone.

This didn't satisfy John and Jed. They knew any reward would be worth a lot more than one hundred dollars, not to mention a fair cut of the find. They told Joey the hundred-dollar bills weren't going to keep them quiet for long. Joey was exasperated, and angry. He again promised to give them each their fair share.

"Look, I'll meet you Saturday night at Dick Lee's, at midnight. I'll give you your cut. After that I don't care what you do. The mafia is in on this. You mention my name or go to the cops and I'll blow your heads off. You go to the cops now, you're dead. If I don't get you, they will."

With that, mindful of the dramatic nature of his threat and caught up in the moment, Joey strutted angrily from the house. Mike walked out after him. They both climbed into the big green-and-white El Dorado, prepared to drive off impressively, but when Joey reached in his pocket for the keys, they were gone. John and Jed came out of house. They watched as Joe stepped back out of the car, swore, and stomped back into the house to look for the keys.

Mike walked over to talk with the boys. He could see how worried and scared they were.

"He's crazy," said John. "There's no talking to him."

Joey finally located the car keys on the backseat of the El Dorado. He dropped Mike off at the Wolf Street house and drove off to pick up Linda and stop by his sister's again. He told Mike he would be back in a couple of hours.

When Mike returned to his house he peeked inside the black suitcase Joey had left in his front closet. It was true! Joey Coyle, he thought, of all people.

6

For Jack Durwood, who worked security for Purolator, the last twenty-four hours had been like a bad dream. How do you misplace more than a million dollars in cash? Was there a worse way of losing it than to have it plop right out the back end of a truck? Where did you start looking for the clown who picked it up?

Durwood was a quiet, balding man of slender enough frame to pose for the "before" picture on a bodybuilding ad, but he was a Vietnam veteran, U.S. Army Special Forces, a man used to being underestimated. Handling security for a company that routinely transported millions of dollars was not the kind of cushy corporate position many military or police veterans fall into at retirement. Durwood had always enjoyed the challenge. But this case was bad. The little they knew only underscored how much they didn't.

Shortly before sunset that afternoon, Durwood got a call at his home in Allentown that shook him temporarily from his doldrums. A guard at the Philadelphia terminal called to say that he had been contacted by someone named Alan David Silverman. He said he was a lawyer; Silverman wanted to talk to someone from Purolator about the missing money. He had left a phone number.

Durwood told the guard to check the telephone directory. There was an Alan David Silverman listed as an attorney. His office was in Center City. So this wasn't just another prank.

Durwood dialed the lawyer. Silverman's wife answered the phone and said her husband would be home shortly. About twenty minutes later, Durwood's phone rang.

"My client has about twenty-five to thirty percent of the missing Purolator money," Silverman said. He also said that his client wanted to return it and that he wanted both his client's name and his own to be kept out of it.

"Do you speak for the company?" Silverman asked.

"Yes, I do."

"I feel that my client ought to be entitled to some kind of a reward." Silverman explained that they would have to work fast, because his client would not have possession of the money for long. His client was "worried and concerned," the lawyer said, because one of the people involved had approached organized-crime figures in Philadelphia about laundering the money.

"Who?" Durwood asked. "Possibly friends of the late Angelo Bruno?"

Silverman ignored the question.

"How did your client come by the money?" Durwood asked.

The lawyer said that his client was not involved in any attempt to keep or launder the money. He said that his client had simply run into "the guy" at a bar early Friday morning.

They had gotten drunk together, and then gone back to his client's home to use drugs. Later, after taking this guy home, his client discovered that "the guy" had left behind his black suitcase. When he opened it he discovered about $300,000 in cash.

Mike DiCriscio had wasted no time. Knowing Joey as he did, hearing the story about Sonny Riccobene, and watching Joey, John, and Jed fighting over what step to take next had evidently convinced him that this whole escapade was going to end badly. Just by driving along with Joey to Masi's house and letting him stash the money in his closet, he could see himself implicated in a criminal conspiracy to keep the money, or answering the door in the middle of the night to find one of Riccobene's thugs. Suddenly the reward money—even just a fourth of it—looked pretty good.

"How did he know it was the missing Purolator money?" asked Durwood.

"I don't know," Silverman said. "I guess the guy told my client that he had found the money."

Durwood told Silverman that his client could earn a percentage of the $50,000 reward by turning in that portion of the money, and that, as far as Purolator was concerned, no charges would be brought against him.

7

Joey's sister, Ellen, had not heard him enter the house. It was after eight in the evening. She heard him calling and walked downstairs. Joey was in the living room, standing in the corner.

"Come here, Ell," he said.

"What's wrong, Joe?"

"Come here. I want to talk to you."

Joey's head was down. When Ellen went to turn on the light, he asked her to leave it off.

"What's wrong?" Ellen asked.

"Come here." They hugged and Ellen could see that her brother was crying.

"What's wrong? Did you get hurt? Are you all right?"

"I'm all right. I'm all right," still hugging her. "You are the only family I have left."

Ellen tried to calm him down. Joey was shaking.

"Look," said Joey. "I got the money."

"What, Joey?"

"I got the money."

"What money?"

"The *Purolator* money."

"Joe, calm down. Let's go have a cup of coffee and relax, take things easy"

"No, no. Stay right here."

"Joe."

"I got the money. I got the Purolator money."

"You do?"

"Yes."

"Why don't you just give it back?"

"Give it back? I can't give it back."

"Why?"

"Don't you believe Daddy had something to do with this?"

"What do you mean?"

"Don't you think Daddy wanted me to have this money, Daddy and God?"

"Joe, *please.* Calm down. Relax."

"Daddy worked so hard all of his life. And for what?"

Ellen had no answers for this kind of talk. She was alarmed. She wasn't sure whether to believe Joey. He was capable of wild fantasies when he was high, as she could see that he was now, high and frightened. As angry as she was with him about taking the drugs, it was a battle too big to fight. So she coped with it, dealt with Joey as she found him. She asked him to spend the night at her place. If he was just freaking out on the drug, she could at least stay with him.

Joey refused.

"Look, I can't stay here. I got to go. There's people after me."

"What people, Joey?"

But there was no talking to him. Now he was up, looking out the windows again, unable to sit still. Ellen was afraid he was going to get hysterical. She kept repeating, "Relax, relax!" Now *she* was crying.

"Look, just don't worry," said Joey. "Everything is going to be all right."

"Joe, I'm worried about you. I don't want anything to happen to you."

"Nothing is going to happen to me. I'm all right. I got protection. I got all the protection I need. Daddy and God is watching over me. See?" and he took a crucifix out of his pocket. It had belonged to his father. Joey had picked it up for luck earlier that day.

"Here," he said, and tore a five-dollar bill in half, handing Ellen one half and stuffing the other in his pocket. "Somebody will contact you and tell you where I'm at and I'm okay, and they'll have the other half of this five-dollar bill."

"Joey, promise you'll call me. Every day. Let me know you're safe."

"Okay."

Then he left.

DAY THREE

Saturday
February 28, 1981

1

After living more than a day in his drugged, excited state, Joey's mind was having even more trouble than usual organizing things. He still wasn't hungry. He had no desire for sleep. He vaguely remembered a promise to meet with John and Jed at Dick Lee's. He was afraid they would back out and go to the cops. He had threatened to kill them if they did, but Joey doubted they would take a threat from him seriously. As confused as he was, he knew he did not cut a very threatening figure.

The death threat had actually frightened him more than it frightened John and Jed. It was as if he had cursed himself, thrown open a door to the dark side of himself, releasing new ghosts of self-loathing and fear. He began to think that maybe the money was not a gift but a curse. He already doubted he would ever see the $800,000 he had given to Carl Masi and Sonny Riccobene, and it occurred to him that they might not just let him keep the $400,000 he still had. But the money was *his!* He now believed that he had been destined to find it, that he had been guided to it by his father, and by God. It gave him a powerful sense of obligation, a determination not to blow this chance. He had this idea that he could use some of the money to swing a big drug deal and some of it to open his own fork-lift repair shop, which would give him work that he liked doing and be a nice cover for the money he made dealing drugs. The potential dizzied him. He would go around to all the big fork-lift dealers and explain what he was going to do; he would re-cruit their business. Then he would outfit the place and employ people. He would make it work out yet. But then he thought about how his father had called him a bum and about what a mess he had made of his life so far, which made the money— *all that money!*—an even heavier burden to bear. So much seemed to be riding on it.

His promise to meet with John and Jed weighed on him so much that at some point Friday night he began thinking that he was to meet the boys *that* night instead of on Saturday. So he had dug out the .44 Magnum he had hidden at home and stuffed it under his belt at the small of his back.

After his conversation with Ellen, Joey picked up Linda in the El Dorado and drove back to Mike DiCriscio's house. The gun dug into his backside uncomfortably on the drive. Mike was waiting with his friend John DiBruno, a short, stocky man whom Joey had never met.

Joey immediately informed DiBruno that he was the one who had found the Purolator money, and produced two crisp hundred-dollar bills.

"Keep it," Joey said, grinning.

Joey was oblivious to it, but his record was perfect. Since the minute he had spotted the yellow tubs by the side of

Swanson, despite his intentions to the contrary, he had told *everyone* he met that he was "the guy who found the money" —his niece, the Masis, Sonny Riccobene, Linda, Mike and Marion, Ellen, and now this guy. He couldn't stop himself. Being "the guy" gave Joey status. He had never had status before, and the opportunity to bask in it was too much to resist. The more people he told, the more his reserve evaporated. Nothing bad had happened so far. Besides, he was planning to skip out for a while, leave the country until things cooled down. He hadn't figured out exactly where or how yet. He had to recover the bulk of the money first. But that was the plan.

One thing Joey didn't do was ponder the implications of his indiscretion. It was reasonable to assume that despite oaths of secrecy, each of these people had probably told one or two others, who had in turn told one or two more. It was only human. And undoubtedly word about the find was now spreading exponentially through South Philly. John and Jed had told their parents, and Mike, of course, unbeknownst to Joey, had already hired a lawyer and contacted Purolator. Joey considered none of this. He was high, excited, and living the dream moment to moment. He also had a strong feeling of destiny, that he had been meant to find the money, that this was *his* moment.

In this frame of mind, the inconvenient fact that John Behlau and Jed Pennock had been with him when he'd found the money was increasingly troubling. He had to get rid of them, scare them off, somehow. Joey wanted Mike and John DiBruno to accompany him over to Dick Lee's for the meeting with John and Jed. Both men were swarthy and Italian-looking. Joey figured that this, and his gun, were all convincing the two younger men would need to keep quiet. He loaded the black bag full of money into the trunk of the Cadillac, and they drove out together across the Walt Whitman Bridge.

Of course, being a day early, they never found John and Jed. They spent hours drinking at Dick Lee's. Joey told the bartender, who expressed some surprise when he kept buying rounds for his friends, "I come into some money."

He then told him he was "the guy," and explained about the Purolator truck and the money bags. Joey, Linda, Mike, and John DiBruno left the bar at closing time and then drove over to Mike's parents' home in Clementon, New Jersey. Joey felt the need to shoot up again.

It was after midnight when he and Linda turned into the curving block of small suburban homes. They were both drunk. Joey had lost Mike's taillights a few blocks back, but recognized the car in a driveway a few houses up. He parked the El Dorado out in front and he and Linda walked across the wet lawn to the front door.

Joey opened the door. Just inside, an unfamiliar man and woman were asleep on the couch. The man leapt up, a short, thickly built man.

"Who are you!" he shouted. He vented a quick, threatening grunt and assumed a karate stance, his hands poised and one leg held high and forward. Joey retreated slowly and reached behind for the heavy pistol stuffed under his belt.

"Who are you?" answered Joey.

"Who are you!" the man demanded.

"Is Mike here?" asked Joey as he backed out the door, confused.

"Who are you?" the man shouted again.

"I'm a friend of Mike's!"

"Who the fuck is Mike?"

The startled homeowner began to back Joey toward the door.

"I made a mistake! I made a mistake!" Joey shouted.

"You're damn right you made a mistake," said the man, who pushed Joey out into the front yard. Joey kept repeating that he had made a mistake, and Linda began shouting the same thing. Then DiBruno appeared and set things straight.

"Look, sorry, I must be at the wrong house," said Joey, whose sudden pleading manner and obvious drunkenness set the man's wife laughing. Then everyone was laughing. Joey had missed Mike's parents' house by two doors.

DiBruno led them to the right house. Mike's parents were asleep down the hall. Mike fixed a pot of coffee and Joey and Linda tiptoed upstairs to a bedroom to shoot up. Joe injected them both with speed, which had a temporary soothing effect on his drunkenness and frayed nerves. He decided to recount the money, laying it out on a bed. When he was finished, he discovered the $400,000 was now just $378,000.

Back downstairs, Joey asked Mike to arrange an investment for him. He wanted to make some kind of real estate deal in Atlantic City, or a drug deal. Mike agreed to help, so Joey stuffed $238,000 in a plastic bag and gave it to him. Mike put it in a closet upstairs.

Joey then decided he needed to apologize for bursting into the wrong house, so he walked out of the DiCriscios', recrossed the wet lawns, and knocked on the door. The karate man answered, looking annoyed again. This time Joey introduced himself, and learned that the karate man's name was Michael Madgey. Madgey invited Joey in. He and his astonished wife fixed coffee in the kitchen, and Joey promptly explained to them that he was "the guy" who had found the Purolator money. He told them how he believed that God wanted him to have it. He told them he had been a driver and bodyguard for Angelo Bruno and Frank Rizzo.

"My father always said I was a bum," said Joey.

The Madgeys felt sorry for him. He seemed so pathetic.

"I don't know about you, but I'm Catholic," he said. "I believe in Christ and God and all that. I believe my father is in heaven with them, and that they meant for me to find the money. And do you know what I plan to do with it? I'm going to give it to people who really need it, old people and kids. I'm really worried about all those kids in Atlanta."

He offered to pay the mortgage on their house. He pulled out a pill from his pocket and asked them if they wanted drugs, "pot or anything." They declined. Then he gave both husband and wife a hundred-dollar bill and left, still holding his cup of coffee.

"Don't spend it yet," Joey said, with a conspiratorial whisper. "I'm tryin' to get to Italy. I'll let you know when I'm there. Then it will be safe to spend it."

As he went out the door, he stooped to kiss Mrs. Madgey on the cheek, and as he walked off she turned to her husband and said, "What an hysterical situation!"

Mike had lost track of Joey during the time he was talking to the Madgeys. He looked around the house for him briefly, then spotted Joey returning across the lawn, holding a cup of coffee and singing.

It was half past four in the morning when Anthony DiCriscio got out of bed. He awoke early every morning. He donned a robe and walked down the hall to the kitchen, where he was surprised to find the lights on, his coffee pot warm, and ashtrays filled with cigarette butts. In the living room was his son Michael.

Mike was on his way out the door. He explained quickly to his father that this "goofy guy" had stopped by with him, and told how Joey had walked into the wrong house. As his son left, Anthony DiCriscio looked out the window. The El Dorado was parked at the curb. A slender blond woman wearing a long coat got in one side of the car. A man with blond hair was behind the car, setting something in the trunk. The trunk closed and the man got in on the driver's side of the car. Then this car and his son's car drove away.

The old man surveyed the mess in his kitchen. On the counter was a half-filled coffee cup that looked unfamiliar.

2

Joey followed Mike's car west on Route 42 toward Philadelphia, but just before getting to the bridge, looking in his rearview mirror, Mike saw the Cadillac turn off near the Camden Marine Terminal.

It was shortly before dawn when the green El Dorado approached the marine terminal, coughed, bounced, and then rolled to a full stop. Joey cranked on the ignition, but the engine wouldn't turn over. So he hiked on to the terminal grounds in search of his older brother, Billy, who worked an early shift. Joey recalled that his brother had a heavy safe at his home in South Philly, which would make a perfect place to put the remainder of his cash. Then he planned to lay low the rest of the day, get back in touch with Masi, and find out what was happening with the $800,000 he had left with him Thursday night.

Billy's shift hadn't started yet, so a friend drove Joey back out to the stalled Cadillac. They fiddled with the engine, jump-started it, and Joey drove back out to Route 42, then back across the Ben Franklin Bridge as Saturday morning dawned in his rearview mirror.

He drove to his brother's house on Second Street and rang the bell. Joe's sister-in-law answered the door. She told him that Billy had already left for work.

"Can I come in?" Joey asked.

"What do you want?" his sister-in-law asked. Relations were strained between the brothers. Joey knew his older brother was disappointed in him and he found it hard to talk to his brother's wife, as if everything he did or said just reinforced an impression of him that was already bad.

"Can I use your safe?" Joey asked.

"For what?"

"Look, I found this money. I want to put it in Billy's safe until I can figure out what to do."

Then Joe opened the black case and showed his sister-in-law the wrapped bundles of hundreds.

She shrieked, "Who did you kill! No, you can't use the safe! Get out of here! Get out of here!" and she shut the door.

Dejected, Joey walked back to the El Dorado, which he had kept running to keep it from stalling.

"We can put it in my sister's basement," offered Linda. "She won't even know."

So they drove to Linda's sister's house on Roseberry Street. Linda slipped downstairs and set the case under the frame of an old, broken stereo.

3

There were so many telephone calls offering so many clues that led in such wildly different directions that by Saturday morning Pat Laurenzi wanted to pull the line from the wall. But you don't do that. You tell yourself it only takes one. You listen politely, ask questions, thank the caller, check out the ones that even mildly bear looking into.

The lost Purolator money was a sensation in Philadelphia. Everybody was talking about it. You couldn't turn on the radio or TV without hearing people laughing and speculating about what they would do with it. Of course, people wanted to know how close the police were to recovering it. Pat's bosses wanted to know, too.

That morning he had at last gotten a call that sounded like a break. A man said that he had driven past the tub on Swanson Street himself, and had seen in his rearview mirror another car stop and pull something from it. It hadn't registered with him at first, but after hearing the news Friday night it hit him. . . . Was there some kind of reward being offered?

Pat drove over to the man's house. It was true, the man had witnessed the money being taken from the street. He verified the description of the car Pat had gotten from the junkyard brothers.

"Did you see the license plate?" the detective asked eagerly.

"I only saw them out of my rearview mirror. I was going the other way," the man said.

He told Pat he thought it had a Pennsylvania tag, but he couldn't recall any letters or digits. Which left Pat right back where he started.

What the detective didn't know was that while he was out, police from across the Delaware River in Gloucester City, New Jersey, had called into South headquarters with another stray bit of information. They had earlier picked up an abandoned car in the 200 block of Mercer Street and reported that it was a '75 Chevy Malibu with blue primer on the right front fender. Pat hadn't considered the find important, because the '75 Malibu looked dramatically different than the '71, which all his eyewitnesses had seen. The Gloucester County police now corrected the earlier report. The car was actually a '71 Malibu.

It was just one more scrap of information, most likely useless. The duty officer walked over to Pat's desk and dropped it on the pile with the hundreds of other message slips he had received that day.

4

J oey and Linda spent most of the day back at the Four
Winds Motel on Admiral Wilson Boulevard. Late in
the afternoon, Joe gave Linda the keys to the El Dorado,
which fortunately restarted, and told her to drive it back to the
neighborhood and return the keys to his friend.

When Linda drove off, Joey walked next door to the French
Quarters Bar, ordered a drink, and then spent the rest of the afternoon trying to reach Carl Masi by phone. When he finally connected, the older man agreed to drive over the bridge to talk. Joey
just wanted to be reassured. He wanted to know where the remainder of his money was, what was happening. He was increasingly convinced that it had been a bad idea to approach the mob,
and he was so nervous about meeting Masi that he told the older
man he was at the Admiral Bar, which was farther down the high-
way, on the opposite side of the road. Joey figured that way he
could watch Masi pull up, make sure he was alone.

He went back to the motel and his stash of speed, and
waited for the appointed hour to meet Masi at the bar. He
watched the sun set outside the window, pacing and drinking.
When it was dark he remembered to call his sister.

"Ell?"

"Yes."

"It's me. Joey."

"What's wrong? Are you all right?"

"Yeah. I'm fine. I can't talk. I'll talk to you later."

And he hung up.

Masi arrived alone. Together they drove down to Atlantic City. Joey had a million questions: Where was the rest of the money? When would he get it back? What was Sonny doing with it? What was the plan? But what Joey was really after were answers to deeper questions: Was Masi really helping him, or ripping him off? Would he ever see the rest of the money again? Was Sonny's organization after him? Should he be as scared as he was? Joey was looking for guidance, but Masi, in that quiet, easy way of his, had few answers. It seemed like every time he asked a question, Masi would ask a question. It frustrated Joey. *That shifty dago bastard,* he thought, but then in the next second he would rebuke himself for doubting his friend.

It was late when they pulled into Atlantic City. The gaming tables at the Golden Nugget were closing, so Joey and Masi treated themselves to a nice dinner and then Joey followed his old friend around as Masi kidded with the waitresses and had a few drinks with some friends. On the way back to the motel, Joey told Masi that he had decided to get the money together and leave the country.

Masi said that Sonny would be getting in touch on Monday. He asked Joey where he would be staying.

"I'll be waiting at the motel," said Joey, but right away the other voice in his head said, *You're crazy, man, you'll be a sitting duck!*

Masi nodded. He tried to calm Joey down.

"Stop worrying. It will be okay."

"Carl, they're after me. They're going to get me."

"They don't know who has the money, Joey. Take it easy."

Joey didn't want to tell his friend that at this point he was less afraid of the police than he was of him and Sonny Riccobene. Masi just kept telling him to calm down, that these things took time. You couldn't break down hundreds of thousands of dollars overnight. Maybe his friend was right. Maybe it was just the drug making him paranoid. Yet if Masi were really plotting against him, isn't that *just what he would say?*

DAY FOUR

Sunday
March 1, 1981

1

Sleep just toyed with Joey Coyle through Saturday night at the Four Winds Motel. He had been going full tilt since Thursday afternoon, through night and day, injecting speed every hour or so in an effort to calm himself. He would lie down on the bed in the motel room and close his eyes and feel his tired muscles twitch. He would awaken from what seemed like sleep and look at his watch and only ten minutes had gone by. Then Joey would crush some more white powder on a spoon, mix it with water, heat it with a match, draw it into a syringe, and inject himself yet again. The ritual required little thought or effort because he had done it so often.

Joey had dreams. He would turn his million into multimillions with big drug deals. It was not so much that he was already greedy for more money. That dream had more to do with pride, with status. Joey's life of addiction for the past year had been a humiliating ordeal of abject dependency, of scrounging for a few more dollars to pay off the dealer, of begging for credit when his wallet was empty and ducking the creditors when bills came due, of falling further and further behind . . . Joey's million would admit him to the other side of the business. He would be the man with all the money and all the drugs.

Users would come to *him*. Joey would use his wealth to send his ailing mother to the best doctors in the world. Instead of being the wayward baby brother, the family bum, he would be the provider, the patriarch, showing up Billy, with his supervisor job on the waterfront. Joey was still stung by the rebuke he had received from Billy's wife. He would use his riches to set up the best forklift repair shop on the Delaware River. He would be the boss.

But Joey's dreams just got tangled up in confusion and fear. In his pocket was about two hundred dollars left over from the check he had received Thursday from the Marine Terminal for the work he had done over Christmas and New Year's. The Purolator money was scattered all over Philadelphia and New Jersey—Joey no longer even knew where most of it was. He could hardly keep track of where it had all gone: $400,000 to Masi and another $400,000 to Sonny Riccobene. How much chance was there that he'd ever see that money again? The more he thought about it, the more convinced he was that the mob would be coming after him for the rest of the find. He had left about $240,000 (Joe wasn't sure exactly how much) with Mike DiCriscio in Clementon, New Jersey, hoping that Mike would sink it in some kind of business deal. About $150,000 was hidden under a broken stereo cabinet in the basement of his girlfriend's sister's house on Roseberry Street. He had handed out hundred-dollar bills—how many? Joe couldn't keep track. Could he trust all these people? Could he trust any of them? People were sometimes gunned down on the street in disputes over twenty bucks! Should he expect all these people to help him keep more than a million?

Four days into his windfall, the money weighed on Joey like a great curse. But the dreams were also strong. This was the one real, God-given opportunity of his life. If he could just see it through.

Very early Sunday morning, Joey called the Masi house and got Dee to drive over the Walt Whitman Bridge in darkness to meet him. Dee took Joey out to a drugstore and bought him black hair dye. Then she took him to the house of his cousin, Joe "Bucky" McCall, a longshoreman who lived in Gloucester.

Bucky had always been Joey's closest relative outside his immediate family. They were the same age, the same size, and their family resemblance was so strong they looked more like brothers than cousins. Joe told Bucky that he had found the Purolator money. He borrowed a clean pair of jeans and a fresh flannel shirt, shaved off his wispy blond mustache, and then treated his thin blond hair with the black dye.

Later in the day, Dee drove him back to her house. Joey sat in the kitchen talking to Carl and Dee. He hoped his fears about Masi were wrong. He found himself returning again and again to the older man's row house for coffee and reassurance. Masi said he had none of the money at his house. He had hidden his portion, and he had not heard from Sonny. Joey learned that Sonny had taken his cut to Las Vegas, where large amounts could be transferred and broken down rapidly.

"Don't worry so much," Carl told Joey. "These things take time."

2

Joey's sister Ellen was washing dishes and her husband, Charlie O'Brien, was watching television when Joey opened the door and walked up the stairs to their apartment.

"Yo!" he said, cheerfully.

Ellen recognized Joey's voice and stepped out into the living room doorway. Ellen and Charlie couldn't believe their eyes. They stared at Joey and then looked across the living room at each other.

"Joe, what did you do to your hair?" Ellen asked.

"I had to change it. I had to disguise myself."

"For what?"

"Look, don't worry about it. I told you about them people. I just had to disguise it. It looks all right, doesn't it?"

It looked terrible. The black dye had stained Joey's neck. Charlie just looked at Ellen and shook his head.

"Sit down, Joey. We'll have coffee," Ellen said.

"No, thanks. No time," said Joey. "Is Mommy up?"

"I guess so. She's watching television with Kathy."

"All right. I'm going to go up and see her."

Joe sat upstairs with his mother and neice for about ten minutes. Then he came back downstairs to the living room and sat next to Charlie. He reached behind him and pulled out the .44 Magnum. Ellen and Charlie were shocked. Joey set the gun down on the coffee table and began disassembling it, poking at it with his handkerchief.

"Are you all right?" Ellen asked.

"Yeah, I'm all right, I'm all right," Joey answered, irritated by his sister's concern.

Ellen had been worried sick about her younger brother since he had stopped in distraught and shaking Friday evening. That was the night he had given her half of a five-dollar bill. Joe still seemed nervous, but less so. Ellen didn't know what to say to him.

"What are you going to do? Where are you going?" she asked.

"Look, can I take a shower here?"

"Yes, sure."

"Can I borrow the car? I want to run home and pick up some clean clothes."

Ellen figured while he was out picking up the clothes and showering she could talk to Charlie, figure out what to do. Maybe Joey would relax after getting cleaned up. Then they could talk, help him out.

Joey left with Charlie's Chevy Nova. Ellen brewed a pot of coffee and got some cake out of the refrigerator.

But Joey didn't come back.

DAY FIVE

*Monday
March 2, 1981*

1

When Detective Pat Laurenzi finished reading the memo his face flushed red with anger. The lieutenant had handed it to him first thing when he came in that morning. Pat walked back to his desk and read it before even pouring his usual morning cup of coffee. He phoned Purolator headquarters to make sure Jack Durwood, its author, was in, and then strode back out of South Division headquarters, got in his car, and drove fast over to the Purolator Company's offices on Swanson Street.

He bounded up the two flights of stairs to the armored car company's executive offices, and searched out Durwood. Confronting the slender, balding company man, Pat could barely contain himself.

"Why wasn't I told about this immediately!" he demanded.

The memo detailed the telephone conversation Durwood had had with attorney Alan David Silverman Friday night. Silverman had called Purolator to inquire about the reward money. It was, frankly, the *only* significant break in the case Pat had been pursuing with such frustration for four days. And he hadn't even been told!

"The lawyer said his client didn't want the police involved," Durwood said. His quiet assurance was completely unshaken by the young detective's anger. "We were trying to work things out and get the money back. We had no contact with the man who had the money, so we don't know who that is. There's nothing you could have done to the lawyer even if you wanted to."

"Not involve the police?" said Pat. "I've got news for you. I'm already involved! How can you keep me out of this?"

Durwood said that the company was more interested in getting the money back than catching up with whoever found it. They didn't want to spook the source.

"Don't you think it would be better for us to handle negotiations like this?" Pat said in a tone that suggested the answer was obvious. "Don't you think we have a little more leverage?"

Pat paced the office as he explained what he had been going through trying to get some lead on more than a million missing dollars in a city of nearly six million people. He had a description of the car that had stopped next to the fallen tub, a vague description of the young blond-haired man who had stepped out and plucked the canvas money bags from it, a few hunches about how the money was probably still in the neighborhood, but beyond that the trail had gone completely cold. Purolator knew how hard Pat was working. They had paid to have the one eyewitness hypnotized, in a desperate effort to wrench an auto license plate number from his strained memory.

Pat was calming down. He could see that Durwood's explanation made sense. But why were they letting him in on it now?

"The deal fell through. Whoever Silverman's client was, he has backed away from the deal, or is holding out for more of a reward. There was nothing more we could do on our own."

Back at South headquarters, Pat asked his lieutenant for permission to have the new witness hypnotized. Not everyone in the department believed in this sort of thing, and Pat wasn't at all sure he did either, but, as he told the lieutenant, "It may be, well, off the wall, but, *maybe . . .* we don't have anything else to go on."

Word passed up through the ranks. The answer came back—"No." The press was panting after this story. The Philadelphia Police Department was not ready to concede that they were reduced to experimenting with hypnosis.

The detective was desperate. He called Durwood, and the company agreed to pay again for another hypnotism.

So Pat picked up Durwood. They fetched the new witness, the man who had seen the bags picked up in his rearview mirror, and drove him to the Center City office of Dr. Howard Pharnes. Pharnes placed the witness in a trance and asked a long series of questions, trying to elicit more details. He was sure the car had a Pennsylvania tag. He could visualize only vaguely, but he felt sure it had the number seven in it, the number seven and the number nine. But that was it.

Pat was disappointed the witness couldn't remember more, but overall he felt good about it. He had done as much with the lead as he could. The digits "7" and "9" weren't much to go on, but they were two new pieces of the puzzle. It felt good to get something new.

2

After leaving Ellen's apartment Sunday night, Joey picked up Linda at the corner outside her sister's house, and they had spent the night together at the Admiral Wilson Motel in New Jersey.

On Monday morning they went shopping at the Deptford Mall, where Joey bought himself new pants, underwear, socks, and a tan suede overcoat.

When he had finished shopping, Joey stopped at a pay phone in the mall to ring Carl to see if there was any news from Sonny. He inserted coins and dialed, but while he waited for the call to go through a man in the overall uniform of the phone company walked up and picked up the phone directly next to his. Joey immediately hung up his phone and walked back to Linda.

"Not home?" she asked.

"No, that guy might be undercover cop."

Linda laughed at him. She told him his paranoia was getting out of control.

DAY SIX

Tuesday
March 3, 1981

1

Frankie Santos did magic tricks. He could do things with a pack of cards in a bar that would have the place buying him drinks all night long.

A lean, dark-haired, dark-skinned young man with a gentle, persuasive manner and big brown eyes, Frank was a charmer, a neighborhood kid with smarts. He had a thick mop of dark brown hair, prominent cheekbones, and a chin that made him appear gaunt. He worked nights and took courses during the day at Camden Community College, collected rare bottles of wine and liquor, and read books and practiced his card tricks on the side so that no matter how many times you saw his act he always seemed to have a new one, already perfected, that you had never seen before. Frank was a traffic controller for the Delaware River Pilots Association, an important and valuable specialty on the river requiring learning and practice, a job demanding precisely the earnest, well-disciplined, responsible qualities Frank possessed. He was a success, the kind of guy who saved his money and invested it, who got ahead in a low-key, steady fashion so that even though you might not have seen him for a year or two, you knew that wherever he was Frank was at least a year or two better off. Still, Frank was not the kind of guy to forget where he came from, who neglected his old attachments and loyalties. Not that South Philly would ever let him.

Frank had lived with Joey Coyle at Joe's mother's house on Front Street for about four months in 1980 after splitting up with his wife. He and Joey were friends going back to Catholic school first grade. Living with Joey had worked out okay for a little while, and Frank was grateful for the favor, but he had outgrown the feckless life Joey was living. Frank couldn't summon the forbearance necessary to stay close to Joey.

For instance, one day when Joey had trouble starting his car, he and his friends had just popped the hood on Frank's car and "borrowed" his battery. They not only neglected to ask Frank's permission, neglected to tell him about it, leaving his inert vehicle parked so that Frank would be surprised by the dull, impotent click of his ignition as he prepared to report for work at midnight. This wasn't just an occasional experience. There was the time Joey and his friends came home drunk one night while Frank was away working on the river and raided his precious store of rare bourbon, old-style bottles of Wild Turkey and Old Forrester with the corks still in them, fancy decanters. It broke Frank's heart. He had bought those bottles from dealers, they were a prized part of his collection. Frank was attuned to layers of subtlety that Joey and some of the old friends from the neighborhood could never quite comprehend. To Joey, a bottle of bourbon was a bottle of bourbon. You killed it when the need was strong and then you replaced it when your pockets were full. It wasn't clear how someone could derive pleasure from a bottle of bourbon without opening it.

Frank found his own place over in Jersey and had moved out. There were no hard feelings. He couldn't stay mad at Joey Coyle for long because no matter how much trouble Joey caused him, Frank knew that Joey meant no harm. There was a helplessness about Joey that made it hard to stay mad at him. After the initial anger subsided, Frank would sometimes actually feel guilty about losing his temper. He found himself going to great lengths trying to explain why those bottles of bourbon were too important to drink, until he began to doubt his own reasoning, as though Joey's pleasure was somehow innocent and his own somehow vaguely corrupt. You knew that if Joey ever had something you needed, he wouldn't quibble if you forgot to ask, or to give it back. Of course, it was hard to imagine Joey ever having anything to take, or give away.

It was early morning, still dark when Frank got the call at work.

"Eh, Frank. It's me, Joe. Look, Frank, I'm in a jam. I gotta talk with ya."

"I'm at work right now," said Frank.

"When are you off?"

"In about fifteen minutes."

"I gotta talk to you."

"Where are you, Joey?"

"Fourth and Butler."

"Okay. I'll pick you up at Sixth and Porter. Fifteen minutes."

Frankie's old red Chevelle pulled up to the corner precisely on time.

"Man, you look terrible," he said as Joey climbed into the car. Joey also smelled terrible.

"I haven't slept in a few days," said Joey, and he launched into a hurried and frightened explanation of how he was "the guy who found the money," how he gave eight hundred thousand to this guy Sonny who was connected, and how the cops were out looking for him with helicopters and dogs . . .

"People are chasing me. They're gonna get me!" he said.

"Joey, look. Calm down."

"I have to get out of the city," he insisted. "You gotta help me. People are chasing me. I still have some of the Purolator money."

"Where is it?"

"Linda is bringing it down here. She should be here any minute."

Joey showed Frank the .44 Magnum he had been carrying uncomfortably under his belt for two days. He had welts on the small of his back from the thing. Joey explained that he wanted Frank to get him on a boat and help him to get out of the country.

"The cops will be watching all the trains and at the airport," Joey said.

Frank just sat behind the wheel with his mouth hanging open. Joey was shaking, hysterical, so frightened that Frank couldn't doubt that the story was true. He had heard, of course, about the missing million. He doubted the business about the mob being involved. Hell, no real organized-crime figure would have let Joey Coyle walk out with four hundred thousand in unmarked bills. Frank knew Carl Masi. He figured Masi was clever enough to have brought in somebody to pose as Sonny Riccobene just to scare Joey into handing over three-quarters of the cash. Frank didn't tell Joey just yet, but he knew right away that the money Joey had handed over was gone, permanently.

They sat there together until Linda arrived with the cash stuffed in socks she was carrying inside her jacket. She climbed into the backseat of the car, removed the jacket, and handed it over. Frank took a long look at the cash, and then at Linda. He figured she was trouble. He didn't know what to do about all this yet, but he knew that if he was going to help sort out this mess, he needed to have Joey to himself for a while.

"Linda, why don't you sit at home for a while and I'll have Joey call you," said Frank. "And don't tell anybody that we're together. Don't tell anybody that he's with me."

"Look, baby, if I make it I'll give you a call," said Joey. "We're going to try to get out of the country."

Frank then drove Joey back to his suburban house in Erial, New Jersey. They laid the money out on Frank's kitchen table and started counting. They counted $119,900.

"Where's the rest of it?" Frank asked.

"It's all here."

"Joe, you told me that you still had about four hundred thousand dollars! There's only about a hundred-twenty here! That's almost two-eighty missing!"

"Linda must have taken some of it."

"Joe! two hundred eighty thousand? Are you sure there's supposed to be four hundred thousand all together?"

"Yeah. She musta took some of it," said Joey, who seemed unconcerned.

Joey didn't mention anything about Mike DiCriscio. He was playing it sly, figuring it was best not to let everyone involved know the whole picture. It gave him his only sense of power over his predicament. Joey figured he was the only one who knew how all the pieces of the puzzle fit together.

"I buried it somewhere," said Joey, but the look in his eye indicated that he had more to tell than that, and after a moment of hesitation, before Frank even had a chance to ask again, Joey began spilling the rest of the story. But he couldn't keep track. He kept confusing people, places, and amounts. Frank stopped him.

"Okay, okay," he said. "Look. Don't tell me anymore. The less I know the better. You tell me the money is buried. Fine. I believe you. Let's leave it at that. The less I know the better off you are, too."

"Okay."

Frank figured the best thing to do was just deal with the money in front of him, since Joey obviously had lost the rest of the million. Clearly, Joey needed some way to keep track of it, so Frank devised a system. He treated Joey like a little boy.

"Look, Joe, why don't you take the money and we'll put it in envelopes," said Frank. He left the kitchen and came back with a stack of white envelopes. "Now count fifty one-hundred-dollar bills and put that amount in each envelope."

As Joey worked at this task, he began again to detail where the rest of the money had gone. He told Frank about Mike DiCriscio.

"You told me you buried that money," said Frank, who was flabbergasted by his friend's carelessness.

Joey just shrugged.

"Joe, tell me, who all knows that you found this money?"

Frank listened first with shock and then with something closer to amusement as Joe labored to list all the names. There were Behlau and Pennock, the Masis, the man called Sonny, Linda Rutter, Joe's niece, his sister and her husband, his sister-in-law Eleanor, most likely his older brother Billy, Mike DiCriscio, John DiBruno, the bartender at Dick Lee's . . .

"*The bartender at Dick Lee's?*"

Joey grinned sheepishly.

Frank shook his head sadly. "Joey, if you have it in your head to keep the money, forget about it. You gave it away to everybody. *Everybody* fucking knows about it. Christ! Even the bartender knows about it! There is no way we can get away with it if we want to try and keep the money. You need to get as much of the money back as you can and go for the fifty-thousand-dollar reward. You need to find yourself a good lawyer and see what can be arranged at this point."

Joey told Frank that he couldn't do that even if he wanted to.

"The mob has got the money, Frank. They'll come after me. They're after me right now!"

Frank doubted it, but he could see that his friend was too frightened to accept calm advice. In any case Joey still wanted to keep the money. He had plans. He still believed he would get most of the money back. At the same time he feared Carl and Sonny, he also stubbornly trusted them, stubbornly trusted Mike DiCriscio. Frank felt in an odd position. On the one hand, he thought he knew what would be best for Joey. On the other hand, Joey had called him for help, had trusted him. Joey was his oldest friend. He felt obliged to help him, even against his better judgment.

"You gotta get me on a ship, get me out of the country," said Joey.

Frank was aware of the risk and complications of doing what Joey wanted. He was willing to help his friend out, but he was not going to place his job and his future in jeopardy.

"Joey, you can't just climb on a ship and leave the country. Why don't you go to Mexico? You don't need a passport to go to Mexico. It would take two or three days at least to get a passport, and they'll catch you if you apply. I don't think there's an extradition treaty between the Unites States and Mexico. If you went to Mexico you could hop on another plane and go to Switzerland or wherever you want to go."

Frank's ex-wife, Laura, worked for the American Express Travel Agency, and he told Joey he would take care of getting a plane ticket. While Joey continued counting, Frank called Laura and explained the situation. He said he thought they should fly out of New York, just in case the cops were watching the local airport. He knew the police had a vague description of Joey. Laura told him there was a nonstop flight to Acapulco from John F. Kennedy Airport in New York City due to depart Wednesday late morning—that would give him and Joey a full day to get up to New York and catch the flight.

Frank asked Joey if he had any identification, like a birth certificate or a voter registration card. Joey said he didn't. Frank reserved one round-trip ticket under his own name. He figured a round-trip ticket would be less likely to invite suspicions of flight, it would look better in case Joey got caught before reaching the plane, and it would give him a way home if things didn't work out for him in Mexico.

Back in the kitchen, Frank collected enough hundred-dollar bills from Joe to pay for the tickets.

"I'll go make the arrangements," Frank told Joey. "You can stay here and wait for me, but stay off the telephone."

Frank drove to his bank and deposited the bills. He then drove into Philadelphia, to the American Express office in Center City, and purchased the tickets from Laura with a personal check. Laura made a reservation for Joey at the Hyatt Hotel in Acapulco. When Frank returned to his house in Erial, Joey was talking on the phone. Frank blew up at him. He threatened to throw him out if he didn't do as he was told.

Joey explained that he had been talking to John Behlau, and that Behlau said he would give him only until eight o'clock that night before calling the cops.

"Well, if you're going to do this, Joe, then we've got to go right now," said Frank. "We'll have to spend the night in New York. Joey, are you sure you don't want to just call a lawyer and negotiate for the reward? Are you sure you want to go through with this?"

"I'm not giving it back," said Joey. "All our lives we've dreamed of something like this, Frank. This is our shot. Why don't you come with me?"

Frank shook his head. "No. I'll help you, but I'm staying. If you want to go, you go alone."

They started preparing to leave. Together Joey and Frank emptied Joey's wallet, took every card or scrap of information with his name on it out to the living room fireplace, and burned it. Frank dug out his baptismal certificate, voter registration card, and other ID and gave them to Joey.

In counting through the bills, Joey had found thirteen that were stamped with a circular "Federal Reserve Bank" emblem that included the date he had found the money: "February 26, 1981." Each had been at the top of a stack when he had originally unwrapped them. Joey gave them to Frank and suggested he burn them. Frank said there was no way he was going to burn $1,300. He told Joey he would just hang on to it.

Frank threw some things together in a bag, and the two were ready to leave when Joey abruptly announced that he couldn't go.

"What!" Frank was growing frustrated. "Why not?"

"Frank, my mom's real sick. What if she gets worse and has to go in the hospital while I'm gone?"

"Isn't she staying with Ellen and Charlie?"

"Yeah, but I got the money, see? I can't just walk out. What if they get me on the airplane?"

Frank understood this to mean that Joe was frightened of being killed by the mob on the airplane.

"Look, Joey, calm down. Nobody is going to get you on the plane. If you're worried about your mom, if you want to leave something for her in case she goes into the hospital, fine. I'll make sure if she goes into the hospital her medical bills will be taken care of."

Joey handed Frank two of the envelopes, $10,000, and then added $4,800 more to cover any expenses Frank might incur while Joey was gone—if, perhaps, Frank might have to fly down to Acapulco himself to bring him back.

Frank said he wanted to put the money somewhere safe. He told Joey again to wait for him and to stay off the phone. Then he drove to his girlfriend's house nearby, and left her with $14,500, all but three hundred of the money Joey had given him and the $1,300 in marked bills. When he got back to the house, he found Joey in the upstairs bedroom, stretched across the bed on his back with his arms folded across his chest over a bag he had stuffed with the money. He held the .44 Magnum in one hand.

"Joey, what do you think, somebody's gonna break in here and rob you?"

"Well, they might," he said.

"You are paranoid, totally," Frank said, and for the first time that day they both laughed.

2

Pat Laurenzi had grabbed a few hours of sleep on top of his metal desk at South Detectives Monday night. Tuesday dawned grim. It had been five days since the money had fallen off the truck.

He had nothing much more to go on than he had started with the previous Thursday, a description of the car, a glimpse of a young man with fair hair stepping out and yanking the money bags inside, and a solid hunch that whoever that young, fair-haired man was, he lived or worked somewhere in the vicinity of Front Street.

Pat was weary and forlorn as he leafed through the thick manila file of leads and notes he had accumulated over the last five days. There were nearly five hundred telephone tips, all transcribed in a variety of handwriting on notes that placed the unknown suspect everywhere from Atlantic City to Texas. The detective had an empty feeling in the pit of his stomach that was more than just hunger.

It was then, deep in the pile of looseleaf notes, that a message caught Pat's eye that he did not recall seeing before. It was from the previous Saturday, the note from the Gloucester City,

New Jersey police correcting their earlier report on the model year of the abandoned Chevy. The Malibu was not a '75 model, but a '71!

Two of Pat's colleagues drove across the Walt Whitman Bridge to Gloucester City to look for themselves. It was a 1971 Chevy Malibu, maroon, blue primer paint on the right front fender. It was almost certainly *the* car.

When Pat got the news, he excitedly typed into the office computer the car's serial number. The computer came back with the information that the car belonged to a John Henry Behlau, who lived at 314 Durfor Street, which was, as Pat imediately realized, not more than three blocks from where the money fell off the truck.

He ran through the precinct and assembled a group of uniformed men to back him up. Then they drove to the house. When he rang the bell a woman answered. She looked at the detective, then at the uniformed officer beside him. Pat identified himself. She didn't seem at all surprised.

"We were wondering when you were going to come," she said.

3

It was about five o'clock in the afternoon before Frank and Joe got under way to New York. Frank made Joe leave his gun behind.

"It's one thing for us to get locked up for having this money," Frank said. "It's another thing if they catch us with the money *and* a gun."

Right away they got lost. They wandered frustrated for about forty-five minutes before they found the New Jersey Turnpike.

Once they found the interstate it was a familiar drive for them. When they were sixteen, and Joey had just gotten his Cinderella driver's license, his learner's permit, they had gone cruising up Broad Street like big shots and picked up two older girls who were trying to get to New York City.

"You want to come to New York with us?" the girls asked.

Frank had looked at Joey. Joey had looked at Frank.

"Sure!" they said, and they had all driven up to New York City that night. Frank and Joey had all of five dollars between them that night, and they dropped most of that on tolls. They drove the girls up to the big city, joking and laughing all they way. The girls made a big fuss about how cute Frankie and Joey were. They figured they had hit the jackpot; their sixteen-year-old heads had spun with vivid, fleshy visions. When they got to New York the girls directed them to a big brownstone hotel, and they all got out together and went in. The girls said they wanted to go out for some drinks. They told Frank and Joey to wait for them in the lobby while they freshened up.

The boys had waited for two hours before realizing they'd been had.

They walked back out to the car. It was a cold night, so they left it running, locked the doors, cranked up the heaters, and tried to get some sleep. At daybreak they were awakened by a beat patrolman rapping on top of the car. They managed to scrape together about fifty cents, and shared a donut and a cup of coffee. The car was almost out of gas, and they were penniless.

Frankie had called his mother. She had a friend who lived in Brooklyn, so Frankie and Joey set off in search of Brooklyn. After a long period of harried trial and error in Manhattan rush hour traffic, Frankie told Joey to pull over. He ran up to a cop directing traffic at a busy intersection, and asked him how to get to Brooklyn. The cop eyeballed the callow youth behind the wheel of the car and asked to see his driver's license. Joey showed him the Cinderella license, which was meaningless in New York State, and both boys had been arrested. Frank's mother's friend kindly showed up to bail them out, bed them down, feed them, and give them enough money for gas and tolls to get home.

That had been more than a decade ago, but Joey and Frank felt some of that excitement rekindle as they drove north with more than $100,000 in cash. Frank told Joey that he at least wanted to stop someplace and buy himself a good suit that afternoon. It was the least Joey could do, with him taking such a risk and all. Joey said sure, but he didn't think Frank was taking any risk.

"Aiding and abetting," said Frank. "That's what I'm doing here. If we get caught now, I'm in just as much trouble as you are."

"What trouble?" said Joey. "I done nothing wrong!"

Then Frank tried explaining to his friend why the money did not really belong to him.

"Hey, possession is nine-tenths of the law!" insisted Joey. "I ain't committed no crime."

Frank explained that, as he understood it, the law required that when you found something of value, you had an obligation to try and return it. If you didn't, you were guilty of theft.

"No way!" said Joey, who knew nothing about law but felt ownership in his bones. "Finders keepers! It's one of the oldest laws there is."

Frank said that might have been the law in the olden days, but that the state of Pennsylvania wasn't run that way anymore. Joey would hear none of it.

They checked into the Sky Line Inn, which Frank picked at random as they drove into Manhattan. Upstairs in the room,

Frank called a service to rent a limo for the night. Joey shot up with speed in the bathroom, and then tried stuffing the envelopes of money into his socks. It wasn't working. He was wearing low-cut boots and high socks, but the weight of the envelopes just pulled the socks down over the boots. Joey wasn't about to leave all the money behind in the hotel room, and he certainly wasn't going to spend this big night on the town sitting in his room, so he ran down to the lobby store and bought some scotch tape. Back up in the room he stuffed half on the envelopes in his socks and wrapped the top of his socks with the tape. It worked fine. Everything was in place. He left the rest of the envelopes in a bureau drawer and stuffed one in his pocket. Since he was in New York, his last night before leaving the country, he and Frank felt safe finally spending a little of it. On his way out, Joey hung a DO NOT DISTURB sign on the handle and stretched a strip of tape over the space between the bottom of the door frame and the door, so he would know if anyone had entered. He was afraid someone from the mob would somehow trace them there. Frank just shook his head. He thought Joey's precautions were comical, but, then again, the intensity of his friend's fear was mildly contagious.

They went outside to wait for the limo, but Joey was impatient so they grabbed a waiting cab and told the driver to take them to Broadway. They explained to the cabbie that they weren't going to see a show but to pick up some girls, so the driver offered to take care of that himself. He took them on a long drive across town, and stopped before a big brownstone on a residential block.

Joey was having second thoughts about this. With all the money taped inside his socks, he realized that he would feel foolish taking his pants off. So he waited while Frank followed the driver inside and went upstairs. Frank was back about ten minutes later, grinning and joking, until he discovered the plane ticket was missing from his pants pocket. He ran back upstairs, complaining loudly that he'd gotten ripped off, but then found the tickets in the envelope on the floor. A woman came downstairs with Frank when he returned. She followed him and Joey out to the cab and got in, offering to give Joey a blow job there in the backseat.

"No thanks. No thanks, baby," said Joey, who squirmed away from her in the seat and fended her off with one arm. Joey was embarassed not to accept, but he was determined not to remove his pants. He reached in his pocket with his free hand, pulled out a roll of hundreds, and presented the woman with one. They left the woman standing on the sidewalk, smiling and waving.

4

Floodlights from a hovering helicopter and from the television crews lined up to broadcast live in front of Carl Masi's house lit up his row-house neighborhood like a movie set. There were reporters knocking on doors up and down the block, pestering neighbors for information about the Masis. Inside, Dee was frantic with worry.

"They are nice people, good friends," said the woman next door, who worried that maybe she shouldn't be answering questions.

A pack of reporters waiting in the alley behind the Masi house saw two women emerge from the house directly behind it. One of the women had a fur jacket clutched around her shoulders. They walked past the reporters, opened the gate to the Masis' yard, and then knocked on the back door. A cop opened it.

"She just called us and asked us to come in," the woman with the fur jacket said.

The cop told them they could not come in.

"She's hysterical in there!" said the woman. "She needs some help. Won't you let us in? She's all alone."

The cop gently shooed them from the door. The women glared at the reporters and photographers who had watched this.

"You people just love other people's tragedies, don't you?"

But this was no tragedy. This was a mystery. The city was now following every twist and turn of the case as the police seemed to be closing in.

Detectives searched every inch of the Masis' house. Uniformed officers milled outside, front and back, sternly keeping the anxious crowd of neighbors and reporters at bay. Word was out that the Philadelphia police had found the missing Purolator million, but from the bustle of activity in and around the Masis' house the case hardly seemed closed. None of the officers on the scene would comment.

Late in the evening the cameras caught a startled Carl Masi, wearing a leather jacket, being led out the front door to a police car. Then a team of detectives emerged carrying green trash bags. It was assumed that the bags were filled with money, but the department's statement just an hour later revealed that none of the cash had been recovered.

It had taken only a few hours from the knock on John Behlau's front door to the evening search of the Masi house. John and Jed were both frightened and angry. After consulting with lawyers that afternoon, and learning that they could not only avoid prosecution but earn some reward money if they helped lead the police to Joey Coyle, they talked freely. They told Pat about finding the money, about bringing it back to Joey's house. They told him how they had urged him to give it back, and how he had instead taken them over to Carl Masi's house. They said Masi

and Coyle and another man—they said they did not know who
the other man was—had split up the money, and that was the
last they had seen of it. At the Masi house the detectives had found
only the remnants of the burned bill wrappers in a trash can on
the patio.

While the searching went on at his row house, back at
South Detective Division headquarters, Carl Masi was feeling
the heat. Still recuperating from open heart surgery, he was
doing his best to stay calm, but he knew he was in more trouble
than Behlau and Pennock. The detectives knew that he had
been given a large portion of the money to hold. To Detective
Laurenzi's anxious questions he gave careful, direct, truthful
answers, but the ex-fighter with the mob connections wasn't
volunteering a thing. Pat told Carl that the only way he could
hope to avoid prosecution was to give back the money, *fast.*

There was a connection between the two men, which
made Carl feel more comfortable. Pat had discovered it from
his father. He had jotted down the name "Massey" after talking to Behlau and Pennock, and noted the alleged mob connection, but the name didn't register with him. Pat was fluent
in the complex neighborhood dynamic of the mob, but this
name had never come up before. So he'd asked his father,
Pasquale Laurenzi. He told his father he'd never heard of the
guy.

"What's the matter with you?" his father had asked.

"What?'

"Spell it," his father said.

"M-A-S-S-E-Y."

"It's not S-S-E-Y, it's M-A-S-I. That's Joe Masi's brother."

Pat had known Joe Masi since he was a kid. A short, thick guy who owned a frozen-food place that made deliveries to his father's store.

When Pat told Carl he was Pasquale Laurenzi's son, it was like a weight lifted from the fighter's chest. He spilled the whole story. He asked Pat to send out for some of his heart medicine, which Pat did. The detective assured him there would be no trouble.

"We just want to money back, Carl."

"It's going to take time," he said.

"You can start right now," Pat said, and pushed a telephone toward him. "Just dial nine for an outside line."

In the meantime—things were moving rapidly now—Pat had sent an all-points bulletin to area law enforcement agencies:

WANTED. JOSEPH COYLE 28 W/M DOB 2-22-53 RES 2323 S FRONT STREET PHILA. PA. 6 FOOT, 150 LBS, DIRTY BLOND HAIR, TATOO ON ONE ARM (SHAMROCK), SCAR ON SIDE OF FACE FROM EAR TO BELOW EYE, FOR THEFT, RSP AND CONSP. SUBJECT WANTED ON WARRANT #98946 SIGNED BY JUDGE LEDERER

Within hours there was a call from Washington Township police in New Jersey. They had arrested one Joseph Coyle in a bar brawl. Pat was busy with Carl, since recovering the money was top priority, so he dispatched two detectives over to Washington Township to pick up Coyle.

There were lots of congratulations going around the office ... Carl was working the telephone hard, trying to contact people and talk them into returning the money ... Pat was feeling the high a detective gets when all the pieces of a tough case begin to fall into place ... Then the phone rang. It was the two city detectives calling from Washington Township.

They had been ushered in to meet Joseph Coyle. He was the right height, the right age, had a shamrock tattoo and dirty-blond hair, only ... no scar. He was the *wrong Joey Coyle!*

5

After leaving the whore on the sidewalk, Joey and Frank asked their cabbie to take them to the best French restaurant he knew. It was late for dinner, but they were seated. Frank made friends with the headwaiter immediately, and invited him to join them. They spent hours there, drinking Dom Perignon, eating pheasant under glass, sampling desserts. They convinced their waiter to join them. With the tips, they left nearly $450 on the table.

It was after midnight when they left. They found a nightclub, but the doorman wouldn't let them in. Frank gave him a hundred-dollar bill, and the doors swung wide. They drank more, and stumbled back out to hail a cab. When they were picked up, neither Frank nor Joey could remember the name or address of the motel they had checked into earlier that night. So Frank told the cabbie to stop in front of a Sheraton. He bribed a clerk at the front desk with $50 to get a room for a few hours and went upstairs to sleep. Joey used the bathroom to mix himself an injection of speed, shot up, and then paced the room nervously, unable to sleep. He had visions of a hit man tracking him down and shooting him in his sleep. Frank complained.

"Man, I don't care what you do, but I need to get some sleep," he said.

Joey wandered downstairs to the garage under the hotel, found an open car door, and curled up on the backseat.

DAY SEVEN

Wednesday
March 4, 1981

1

A t dawn, hundreds of thousands of newly printed newspapers were being distributed throughout Philadelphia bearing headlines and stories announcing the arrest of Joey Coyle. The paper had gone to press before the police discovered they had arrested the wrong Joey Coyle. The stories that morning told cheerful tales of the unemployed South Philadelphia longshoreman who had given away a fortune to seemingly everyone he met, and predicted the imminent recovery of the lost Purolator million.

BAR BRAWL YIELDS A SUSPECT IN SEARCH FOR $1.2 MILLION

"I can't talk," John Behlau told reporters who came knocking at his door. "My lawyers told me not to say anything." He seemed happy.

Down the street, Jed Pennock was even more abrupt, saying, "Sorry, pal. No comment."

Meanwhile, Frank Santos was waking up in a hotel room in New York City with Joey peering over him impatiently.

They had about four hours to find the Sky Line Inn, retrieve the remainder of the money, and get Joey to John F.
Kennedy Airport in time for the 10:45 flight to Acapulco.

Frank dressed quickly. He and Joey stopped at a shop
inside the Sheraton to buy a Joey a twenty-five-dollar bag filled
with toiletries. Neither of them had ever been to Mexico, and
Frank figured it was stuff he might not be able to get easily in
Acapulco. Frank bought one for himself, too. Joey picked out
an expensive pair of sunglasses for himself. Then they went out
and hailed a cab.

Neither Joey nor Frank could remember the exact name
of the hotel they were looking for. Joey blamed Frank and Frank
blamed Joey. Finally, exasperated, Frank explained to the cabdriver how they had arrived at the "Sky something-or-other"
the afternoon before.

"We just came straight on through the Lincoln Tunnel
and veered off toward the left," he said.

The cabbie frowned. He drove what seemed to Frank an
extremely roundabout route in the general direction Frank described, but there was no sign of the motel. Joey, who was even
more nervous than usual, lit up a cigarette. The driver turned and
asked him to put it out. Then Joey and the cabbie started to argue.

"Just let us out right here!" shouted Frank. He paid that
driver impatiently, with Joey pacing the sidewalk behind him,
cursing the guy. They hailed a second cab. This driver was Ira-
nian, and only barely understood Frank's attempts to describe
their destination. He drove for about twenty minutes before
Frank decided it was time to try someone else. They paid the

cabbie and stepped out to the curb again. But as the taxi pulled away, Joey said, "Oh no! I left my bag in the backseat."

Frank took off after the cab on foot, waving and shouting. He chased it for two blocks before catching it at a red light. As he walked back to Joe with the retrieved bag of toiletries, Frank upbraided himself for being such an idiot. Here they had some $100,000 in cash, most of it squirreled away a motel they couldn't find, the Philadelphia police, the FBI, and God only knows who-all else chasing them, a plane to catch all the way across the largest and busiest city in the world, and he was wasting time and energy sprinting after a cab to recover twenty-five dollars' worth of toiletries in a bag. Frank threw them at Joey when he got close enough.

The third cabdriver, an older man, found the motel. He knew right away.

"Near the Lincoln Tunnel?" he asked. "That would be the Sky Line Inn."

Frank didn't want to lose this cabdriver, who both spoke English *and* seemed to know where he was going in Manhattan, so he told Joey to wait for him while he ran into the Sky Line Inn to retrieve the money. Up in the room, stuffed in the drawer with the envelopes of cash, Frank found a plastic bag with almost half a pound of drugs. He knew it would be crazy to send Joey out of the country with that, so he flushed the contents down the toilet and pushed the envelopes into the empty bag. Joey would be pissed, but it was for his own good. Before leaving the room, Frank grabbed a pad of stationery and a pen from the dresser top.

Back in the cab, he told the driver to get them to the airport as fast as he could. He handed Joey the bag and then signed his own name on top of the pad and handed that to him.

"Here, practice signing my name," he said, "just in case somebody challenges your ID at Customs."

As the cabdriver fought his way through morning rush hour, driving into the early sun, Joey went to work in the backseat signing "Francis Santos" over and over again on the page.

They arrived at the airport shortly after nine-thirty. Joey went to the men's room to shoot up and to stuff the remainder of the envelopes inside his socks and boots and pockets. Frank went to check in and get a seat assignment.

Joey was having trouble making all the money stay put. The envelopes pulled at his socks uncomfortably. He was worried they would spill out of his boots. Joey had an idea. He strode out to a sales counter and bought panty hose. Back inside the men's room, closed in a narrow stall, he wrestled off his pants and boots and socks, stacked the money on the floor, and then squirmed into the panty hose. This was a new experience for Joey, and it was hard pulling the hose on. They yanked at the hairs on his legs. Once he'd stretched them on he lowered them again and began stuffing money in the panty hose, first packing the lower part of his legs and then pulling them up to stuff more around his thighs. The hose held the envelopes tightly in place. Joey had his pants in one hand and the waist band of the panty hose in the other. He looked down at his legs in the hose and felt a brief surge of panic. How was it going to look if he got caught, or if some hit man got to him on the plane? Joe could imagine the humiliation, even posthumously, of being found wearing a pair of panty hose. Would people understand? The idea gnawed away at him until he couldn't stand it anymore. So he reversed himself quickly, pulled off the panty hose, pulled on his socks, stuffed some of the envelopes in them, pulled on his jeans again, got in his boots, and stuffed more of the envelopes inside his boots and stuck the remainder in his overcoat pockets. He would just deal with the risk. On his way out the door he stuffed the panty hose, which he had balled tightly in his fist so no one would see, deeply into a trash can.

Frank was waiting for him nervously outside the men's room door.

"What the hell were you doing in there?" he asked, but he didn't wait for Joey to explain. He directed Joey across the airport to the designated gate. Once there, Frank handed him the folder with the tickets and showed him where to stand in line to check in for the flight. Attendants were announcing that boarding would begin shortly.

As Joey took his place in line, two tall middle-aged men in business suits strode directly up to him.

"Is your name Joseph Coyle?" one of the men asked.

"Yes," said Joe reflexively. Out of the corner of his eye he could see other men approaching Frank.

The man held out one hand and flipped open his wallet to display a badge, and as the other man took strong hold of Joey's upper arm the man with the badge said, "You're under arrest."

"Oh, shit," said Joey. "FBI."

2

Of course, right from the beginning one of the most likely scenarios Pat Laurenzi could envision for whoever found the Purolator money was for him to flee the country with it. But until he knew who had the money, there was little he could do with that hunch short of asking local airline offices and travel agencies to watch for customers buying tickets with hundred-dollar bills.

Once he had learned the name Joey Coyle late Tuesday, though, the detective had something more to work with. At the same time he was overseeing the apprehension of Carl Masi and debriefing of John Behlau and Jed Pennock, other detectives were dispatched to find out as much as they could about Joey Coyle.

Ellen O'Brien, Joey's worried sister, tried not to be too helpful. She felt her first loyalty was to her brother. Truth was, Ellen didn't know where her younger brother was or where he had hidden the money. So she played along. When the detectives asked to search her apartment, she said, "Sure, but you won't find anything." And when one of the cops asked her to name some of Joey's best friends, she couldn't see any strong reason not to. One of the first names that occurred to her was that nice young man who worked as a river pilot named Frankie Santos.

It was late on Tuesday night, with Carl Masi still making his worried phone calls, when they discovered Frank Santos had purchased a round-trip ticket to Acapulco from JFK Airport in New York, due to depart the following morning. That information had been sent to FBI headquarters in New York City, along with a thorough description of Coyle.

FBI Special Agent Walter F. Yoos and his partner, Agent James J. Malley, had had to look twice when Joe stepped up to the ticket counter. The man they were looking for was supposed to have a mustache and dirty-blond hair. This fellow was dressed in a new tan sport coat and tan slacks, his hair was brown, and he had no mustache. But there was no hiding that scar. It pulled the whole right side of Joe's face off-kilter.

The Purolator money had begun returning a few hours before Joe and Frank were arrested. As Carl continued making phone calls from behind Pat's desk at South Detective Division through the night, the detective took a call that directed him to an open lot on Delaware Avenue just north of Washington Avenue. The caller explained that it was a wide-open area—it was not far from where the money had fallen off the truck six days before—where both the detective and the caller could be confident they were alone. Pat parked his stock blue Chrysler in the middle of the road. He watched his breath dissipate against a metallic morning sky as he sat on the front hood of his car, waiting. At the appointed time a car drove up next to his, and a man rolled down the window.

"Are you Laurenzi?" he asked.

"Yes."

The man dropped a yellow-and-black plastic bag out the window and drove away. The bag had "Fabulous Las Vegas" written on the side; it looked to Pat like something you might buy at a souvenir shop there. In it was $381,700.

Later on Wednesday, attorney Dennis Eisman handed over $229,300 to police headquarters at 8th and Race Streets. Eisman was representing Mike DiCriscio, to whom Joey had turned in an effort to invest a substantial portion of his find.

Pat made another pickup the following morning. It had been a happy day. Waiting for more of the money to come in, Pat played with the hundreds on his desk. It took up a suprisingly small amount of space for so much money, he thought. Stacked neatly, it was about a foot square and about four inches high. The detective amused himself by making a little pyramid out of it.

He had gone home to Roxborough early Wednesday evening to try and get his first night's sleep in days, and had laid down like a zombie on his living room couch when the phone rang calling him back into the office. He was to expect another call in an hour at his desk. The detective drove back to South Philly, rolled his jacket into a ball, and used it as a pillow as he lay down on the desk. He was awakened by a caller directing him to a meeting at Washington Avenue and Water Street.

At five in the morning, streetlamps illuminated the new falling snow. It would fall steadily for twenty-four hours, such an accumulation that the detectives dispatched to New York City to pick up Joey and Frank would be stuck there overnight.

Pat waited on the hood of his car. A car approached. A man rolled down the window and pointed toward a bush, then drove away. Behind the bush was a wet, brown grocery bag covered with a layer of snow. Inside the bag was $267,800.

In New York City, the FBI counted 1,052 hundred-dollar bills stuffed in Joey's socks, boots, and pockets. They found forty-eight on Frank. His girlfriend turned over one hundred and forty-five. Linda Rutter turned in one she had skimmed off the top of a pile as a souvenir. Two more came from the Madgeys, the Clementon, New Jersey, couple whose house Joey had stumbled into accidentally two days after finding the money.

When the fancy money-counter loaned to Pat by Purolator was finished counting, more than a million dollars had been recovered. Somewhere out there was still $196,400. Pat suspected it wasn't coming back. It was a reasonable bargain. You drop $1.2 million off the back of a truck in South Philly, and sixteen percent was a fair price for getting it back.

Who had that sixteen percent was anybody's guess. Pat guessed most of it had been lost in Las Vegas casinos.

3

etting arrested gave Joey an unexpected sense of relief. Granted, it was the end of his big-shot fantasy —Joey the smooth drug dealer, owner of his own forklift shop empire —but it was also the end of worrying about hit men. It was only after his arrest, when he came down off the weeklong high, that Joey realized how much the fear had outweighed the fantasy.

Carl Masi denied, of course, that the mob had ever been involved. Frankie Santos protested disbelief that anyone connected with "organized crime" could have played a role in Joey's bumbling efforts to keep the Purolator money. In all the statements given to the FBI and police, in all the testimony that would later be recorded in Joey's weeklong trial, no one named the man called "Sonny." Mario Riccobene just vanished from the story, like the $196,400.

When he was first interrogated in New York by the FBI, Joey refused to reconstruct his crazy odyssey. He was apologetic, but firm.

"I don't think I'd better talk about it," he told the four unfamiliar FBI agents sitting around him. Joey explained that if he talked, it would destroy his reputation back in the neighborhood for life. "I got responsibility to my friends," he said. "They were just tryin' to help me, doin' me a favor. Hey, I'm only human. Until last Friday I couldn't even count to a thousand. If Purolator was givin' the money away, I thought I'd give it a try. Ain't no crime in that." He was doing his best to charm the stone-faced FBI agents.

The agents put it plain. Unless the money was returned—all the money—there was a crime, and Joey was in big trouble.

"But if I tell you where the money is, I'll have to give up my friends!" protested Joey.

"Maybe there's a way you could turn in the money without involving your friends," one agent suggested.

Joey was wary. He asked whether he could talk to Frank privately. So the agents left Frank and Joe together for a while. Frank urged Joey to do whatever he had to do to protect himself.

When the agents came back, Joey asked to make a phone call. He said he would try to talk his friends into contacting the Philadelphia police anonymously and turn the money in. First, Joe called Dee Masi at the Fidelity Bank, but she wasn't there. Then he found her at the house. Dee told him that the police had already come, that Carl was cooperating with them, that Behlau and Pennock had given up his name and were negotiating for a reward, and that some lawyer for DiCriscio had turned in a chunk of it. As Joey would later put it, "I felt like a slapped ass." He hung up the phone, stunned.

"I'm somethin'," he told the agents. "While I'm here stallin', tryin' to figure out how to keep my friends out of it, they're all turning the money over and fingering me!"

Joey proceeded then to tell his story as best he could. He hadn't shot up for several hours, so he was beginning to feel woozy and afraid. He remembered clearly finding the money, and he recalled vividly some of the things that had happed in the tumble of days and nights that followed, like visiting Mike DiCriscio's parents' place in New Jersey and stumbling into the wrong house, and screwing Linda Rutter and driving down to Atlantic City that night with Carl Masi, but when Joe finished his story was just a jumble of scenes out of sequence. There were big gaps. For instance, as Joey remembered it, he had called Frankie on Sunday, and they had driven up to Manhattan the same day and spent one night in a hotel.

"That can't be right," one of the FBI men said.

"Why not?" Joe seemed genuinely surprised and disappointed.

"Because if you only spent one night in New York, that means we arrested you Monday."

"Right!"

"But this is Wednesday."

"Oh."

4

With snow stalling traffic in and out of Manhattan, it was Thursday afternoon before Detectives Martin Mikstas and Jake Morrison were able to pick up Joey and Frank from lockup and drive them back home. They were happy to be leaving, even if it did mean they were heading back notorious to face the music. Joey said he was particularly happy to be leaving New York City.

"You don't like New York?" Mikstas asked.

"I'd rather be in Philly," said Joey.

"Why?"

"Bad memories," said Joey.

They complained to the detectives that they were hungry, so Mikstas steered to an Interstate 95 rest stop to get some chow. Between them, Frank and Joey had one dollar and twenty cents—exactly one one-millionth of the money Joey had found, Morrison noted dryly. The detectives bought them hamburgers.

"Bet they taste like a million," said Morrison.

Later, as they exited I-95 at Tasker Street, Mikstas had to slow down and steer around a big box lying on the road.

"Hey, Joey, want to step out and see what's in there?" Mikstas asked.

"Fuck you," said Joey.

THE TRIAL

1

Joey Coyle came home a hero. Nobody was more surprised than he was. The headline in the *Daily News* read:
RICH MAN POOR MAN.

Featured on the front page was a full-length shot of Joey arriving in court, his rakish, long raincoat flapping open, his hair dyed, wearing the pair of orange aviator sunglasses he had picked up at Kennedy airport waiting for his flight.

The newspaper called him "romantic" and "a folk hero." The *Philadelphia Inquirer* described him as "handsome, friendly, well-liked by the ladies, never in trouble with the law." Ellen could hardly recognize her sad, mixed-up, ne'er-do-well little brother in the reports she read and heard.

What was going on? Sometimes real life veers just close enough to fable that it is hard not to let fantasy finish the picture. Newspapermen were closet romantics anyhow, most of them. They hid it beneath a crusty veneer, wrapped themselves in hard experience, but one of the things that kept reporters out there looking for stories every day, year after year, was a belief in miracles, in the stubborn viability of goodness, in the ultimate triumph of the little guy. And if you had to look past a few things when the story was too good to be true . . . well, you did. So there was no mention in the stories of Joey's addiction, of his frequent minor scuffles with the law. What the media had on its hands was an urban folk tale, so to fit its contours Joey's rougher edges had to be smoothed. He didn't mind that much at first. He particularly liked being portrayed as a ladies' man, although he knew that much of it was pathetically untrue. He had always been inept with women, and they inevitably saw him for what he was, helpless, impulsive, addicted, addled. But he did his best to keep up the new appearance. He started dressing snappier, and there was a new swagger in his stride. Reporters called from all over the country trying to get a word with him, but his new lawyer, A. Charles Peruto Jr., had given strict instructions for Joey not to say a word. He didn't have to. There was a chorus of praise in his defense. The neighborhood rose up mightily to protect its own. You would have thought he was the greatest man to have been born in South Philly. Neighbors took up a collection to post bail for Joey and Frank. In short order Joey Coyle was a modern Robin Hood, the lucky, likable kid from down the street, Everyman, desperately trying to share his good fortune with the whole wide world.

"He gave $100 bills to friends and strangers alike, bought drinks for the bar at several taprooms," the *Inquirer* reported. the *Daily News* wrote, "It does seem as if the storybook tale of a poor but popular man stumbling on unheard-of riches has captured many an imagination." Joey's friends, who had collaborated to turn him in, now made up for their betrayal with praise.

"If they need character witnesses for Joey, there won't be a courtroom big enough to hold them," said Mike DiCriscio. "I have a nickname for him—the Millionaire—because he would give you the shirt off his back."

"I don't think he was a hero, but I felt sorry for the guy," said Michael Madgey, the man whose house Joey had stumbled into drunk the week before. "It was just a hard-luck case. He had this one big break in his life and he blew it."

Mrs. Madgey was still charmed by the late-night encounter.

"It wasn't a bad experience," she said. "He did nothing bad to us. If I could say anything that would help him, I would. He was just so nice."

Even the FBI got in on it.

"Everybody has a little sympathy for him, I'm sure," said Agent Mike Wald.

A store in Center City called The T-Shirt Museum was doing such a business in "Free Joey Coyle" T-shirts that Joey stopped by to sign the inventory.

"We all love bunglers," wrote *Daily News* columnist Jill Porter, who nevertheless faulted Joey for not giving back the money. "It is said there isn't a jury in the world that would convict him."

When Joey appeared for his arraignment on that first day back in Philly, wearing a sport coat over a silky black shirt open to his belly and sporting a gold necklace and amulet, hundreds of well-wishers jammed the small courtroom in the basement of police headquarters, so many that they spilled out into the hall. They cheered and shook his hand and patted him on the back as he entered. The judge took the unprecedented step of allowing TV cameras in the courtroom to broadcast the proceedings.

Assistant District Attorney Robert Casey argued that Coyle wasn't a folk hero; he was a thief. The law in Pennsylvania was clear. If you found something of value greater than $250, you were obliged to make an effort to find its rightful owner. In this case, given the publicity around the loss of more than a million dollars, there could be no excuse for Coyle's failure. It was theft, conspiracy to commit theft, and receiving stolen property. Given that the defendant had been arrested waiting to board a plane to Acapulco, he was definitely a flight risk, and there was still almost $196,400 missing!

The young prosecutor was earnest but completely out of touch with the mood of the proceedings. Joey's lawyer, Peruto, played to the crowd and camera.

"This isn't organized crime, your honor," he said. "If anything, it's *disorganized* crime. There was no criminal intent. My client is a practicing Catholic, a man who lives at home and cares for his elderly mother. He's never even had a brush with the law." Peruto emphasized that Joey had found the money, not stolen it. He was guilty of getting a little carried away. "The facts suggest that he may be as honest as some politicians," Peruto said.

Judge Mitchell Lipshutz was clearly unimpressed with the state's case.

"Your office had an obligation to better prepare this case," he reprimanded Casey. Pennsylvania law says that those who find large sums of money must take "reasonable steps" to return it, but that using the money temporarily is not necessarily theft, the judge said. Lipshutz complained that Casey had presented no evidence that Coyle had planned to flee with the money, or even intended to keep it. He released Joey on bail, and ordered both lawyers to file written motions. Weeks later Judge Lipshutz dismissed all charges against Joey.

But the state wasn't going to give up that easily. Casey reentered the charges immediately, this time defining them more clearly. Joey was charged with theft and with "theft by failure to return property lost, missing, or stolen." The penalty was three and a half to seven years in prison.

Joey's lawyer counterattacked. His client, he said, had been driven temporarily insane when he found the money. The episode had destroyed his client's life. In fact, Peruto said, Joey was considering suing Purolator for "mental suffering."

"They're idiots," the lawyer said. "It's their neglect that brought all the problems on Joey Coyle. It's their ridiculous stupidity."

2

It was hard to find a jury to sit in judgment of Joey Coyle. Philadelphia's body politic seemed to feel the "crime" fell into a morally gray area, perhaps into that small place reserved for the larceny in everyone's soul. Who among us, no matter how virtuous our intentions, could withstand a truly spectacular, unsolicited temptation? And, in this case, who was the victim? The Federal Reserve Bank? That was a giant modern building in Center City, a great gleaming monolith, a perfect symbol of power in the abstract of vast uncountable national resources. One-point-two million dollars to the Federal Reserve Bank was like crumbs at the bottom of an empty pocket. And Purolator. What was that? A corporation that moves billions every day, very likely insured to the hilt. It was a sure bet that Purolator, in the end, hadn't lost a penny. The only victim, once you thought about it, was Joey himself. Who had been arrested. Whom the state was trying to lock away for three to seven years.

Joey's press had painted him as a romantic, rakish figure. One reporter said that the scar drawn across his face made him look "as jaunty as a pirate." He was just the happy-go-lucky goof who had found the money and done such a laughably bad job of trying to keep it. Of course, Joey had never actually gone around handing out hundreds out of the kindness of his heart, it had been more in the spirit of encouraging people to keep their mouths shut. Even the Madgeys had been given hundreds as an apology. Joey had his happy-go-lucky side, sure, but he had a dark side as well, and the sudden dose of celebrity drove him deeper into it. He was afraid of going to jail, and when his mother died on Mother's Day, just weeks after his arrest, he was convinced her worry over him had caused it. Now he was walking around with guilt over both of his parents' deaths, and he was once more penniless so the speed, which was his balm, was hard to get. The celebrity made it all worse. Joey just wanted everybody to leave him alone, to stop asking him where he had hid the missing $196,400, to let him go back to being anonymous. He wasn't comfortable as a hero because he didn't feel like one. He felt terrible. Weeks after his mother's death he had slashed at his wrists with a razor. He hadn't done serious damage, but when mention of the suicide attempt hit the newspapers it was the first hint that the public image of Joey Coyle wasn't the complete story.

Still, Joey was a popular figure, which made finding an objective jury difficult. Judge John J. Chiovero convened the trial on February 16, 1982. The judge was a lean middle-aged man with a lined, world-weary face. He began by questioning prospective jurors. One of those brought before him was Cheryl Deppenschmidt.

"Is it Miss or Mrs.?" the judge asked.

"It's Mrs., but I'm divorced."

"You indicated that you either heard or read something about this case?"

"Yes, your honor."

"How long ago was that?"

"I would say more than a year ago."

"I see. Do you recall what you heard or read?"

"Yes."

"What was it?"

"In detail?"

"You may tell the court what it is."

"What I recall is that a Purolator truck apparently dropped a bag of money, which was picked up by someone who was Mr. Coyle, and the funds were not returned to Purolator."

"I see. Is that all that you can recall?"

"I recall that Mr. Coyle was apprehended at the airport in New York by federal agents."

"I see. All right. The fact that there was a Purolator truck involved and that money was recovered by Mr. Coyle and retained by him is not a fact that is going to be denied in this case. In spite of what you have read and in light of what I have just told you, can you put aside what you read anyway and adjudicate this matter in a fair and impartial manner based on only the testimony which is elicited in this courtroom and the evidence presented in this courtroom?"

"Adjudicate?"

"Decide. Sorry. Can you do that? Do you have a fixed opinion about the guilt or innocence of Mr. Coyle?"

"I think I do. Yes, your honor."

"You do. And that is a fixed opinion based on the fact that Mr. Coyle recovered the money and retained it for himself?"

""Yes, your honor."

"As I told you, that is a fact not denied by the defense in this case. The defense is alleging insanity, and there are other factors to be considered by the jury. Would you be able to consider those other factors and be fair and impartial and objective in that respect?"

"I would like to think that I could, your honor. I am not positive that I could."

"You are not positive."

Mrs. Deppenschmidt went on to explain that she was not all that surprised by Joey's moves after finding the money, but said she would be willing to try to be fair-minded about weighing the evidence. But pressed to answer whether she could give the matter a full and fair hearing, she finally confessed that she didn't think she could. She was dismissed.

Then came a Thomas Bugeida, who said he had heard plenty about the case, and that he had a strong opinion about the matter already.

"Based on all the knowledge that I have up to this date, and the opinion I have formed, I don't really think that I would change it," he said.

Bugeida was dismissed. Then came James Mellor.

"Good afternoon, Mr. Mellor," said the judge.

"Good afternoon."

"Mr. Mellor, . . . you indicated that you had some preconceived notions about this particular crime, is that correct?"

"Yes, sir."

"Will you please advise the court of exactly what that is?"

"I figured I'd do the same thing in his situation."

"Mr. Mellor?"

"I figure if a man doesn't have no money all his life and finally gets some, he could go a little insane with it."

"I see," said the judge. "I certainly appreciate your candor, Mr. Mellor. That's a very honest answer. We appreciate that very much."

"You're welcome," said Mellor. He was dismissed.

Then there was Martin E. Fosque, a disheveled-looking gentleman.

"Mr. Fosque, good morning," said the judge.

"Good morning."

"Mr. Fosque, you indicated that you could not be fair when I questioned the panel of prospective jurors. Is that correct?"

"That's probably correct, your honor."

"Is it correct?"

"Yes, it is."

"I am shocked. I can't believe that one of our citizens could not be fair in adjudicating a matter in a court of law. Could you please explain that to me?"

"There is so much about the case—there is so much that I have read and seeing so much about the case, from me being a street person, I might have did the same thing myself. Who knows? Or I might have give the money back. So I wouldn't say. I couldn't really be fair about it. I couldn't be fair to the court."

Mr. Fosque was excused.

There was Paul Vettraino.

"Mr. Vettraino, in response to my questioning of the panel as a group you indicated that you either heard or read something about this case, is that correct?"

"That's correct."

"How long ago was that?"

"All through. I have been following it all through since February."

"What is it you recall about the case?"

"Well, the money fell off the back of the truck."

"Right."

"One-point-two million dollars off the back of a Purolator truck and it was recovered by Mr. Coyle."

"Right."

"And he got caught going on an airplane to New York with the money in his boots."

"Right."

"And that's about it, I guess. That's all I can remember."

"That's about it, I see," said the judge, who explained that the basic facts of the incident were not in dispute. "So that if you have any fixed opinion about that, it is of no real consequence because there are other factors in this case that must be considered before a determination, a proper determination can be made of the guilt or nonguilt of this defendant. Do you understand?"

"Right."

"Now, based on what I have told you and considering all that you have read and understand about the case, can you be fair and objective in making an adjudication in this matter as to the guilt or nonguilt of this defendant?"

"Adjudication?"

"Sorry. Decision."

"Well, personally, I feel he is more or less closer to the same financial predicament that I am. I am liable to do the same thing. That's why . . ."

"That's why, what?"

"Deeply inside I don't feel really qualified because of the compatibility between our financial predicaments. I was unemployed for a while."

"You think that you would have done the same thing. You can't dismiss that from your mind even upon the court's instructions?"

"I was up all last night. I was thinking about it last night and the same thing. In all honesty, I really cannot say I wouldn't have done that."

"You couldn't dismiss that from your mind and be fair?"

"I would find it very difficult."

Vettraino was dismissed.

Joey, meanwhile, was not making a good impression on the judge. On the afternoon of the first day of jury selection, he wandered into the courtroom about half an hour after the session had begun. Judge Chiovero beckoned him to the bench.

"Good afternoon, Mr. Coyle. Mr. Coyle, I notice that you were late for court this morning. You were late again this afternoon."

"Yes, sir. I had to shoot down to the hotel and get changed."

"Pardon?"

"I shot down to the hotel that I am staying at and had to get changed. I tried to get back."

"I tell you that because I want to impress upon you the importance of being punctual during the entire period of the trial. Do you understand?"

"Yes, sir. I am sorry. I apologize."

3

It took three days to select a jury. It convened on February 23, 1982, three days shy of a year after Joey had found the money. It took place in one of the grand but seedy courtrooms inside City Hall, the ornate French Second Empire structure that sits on an island at the center of the intersection of Center City's main roads, Broad and Market Streets. Traffic flowing in both directions is forced to navigate around City Hall, assaulting its gray walls with a ceaseless din. The hall's antique heating system at midwinter could warm the old courtroom to a swelter, so judges often had to choose between battling the din or suffocation. Judge Chiovero kept the windows slightly open. He had finally assembled a jury of eight women and four men. Only one of the jurors was a college graduate. Three of them were in their twenties, and two were elderly. The jury was half black, half white. Only one juror lived in South Philly, a bus driver.

Robert Casey would prosecute Coyle. He was a fair-haired, crisp young man with an easy, professional manner. Casey had been in the district attorney's office for several years, long enough to have been battered by the unrelenting tide of real-life horror stories in

Philadelphia's criminal courts, yet he retained a hint of starch and zeal. The necessary capacity for moral outrage hadn't been beaten out of him completely. In the year since his arrest, Joey had retained the services of veteran trial lawyer Harold Kane, a short, cocky, well-dressed man with street smarts and an avuncular style. Kane wore his hair a little long and had a mustache, and formed a contrast with the prosecutor that worked to Joey's benefit right from the start. Beside the defense lawyer, Casey tended to look prim, like a snitch, like the kid who would raise his hand to inform on the other kids in class. Kane was easygoing to a fault. He had the seen-it-all, shockproof good humor of the classic defense lawyer. He spoke with a working-class Philadelphia accent, and had a generous, forgiving manner.

Ralph Saracino, almost a year removed from his job as a guard and driver for Purolator, described the steps he and his partner, William Proctor, had taken that fateful day. They had started that morning in Pennsauken, New Jersey, and had spent the morning driving around dropping off and picking up money from banks. They then delivered the money they had collected to the giant Federal Reserve Bank building, where, on most work days, they picked up the money they would deliver to banks the next morning.

Saracino described his routine. He would inspect the money bags for any tears or fraying and then inspect the seal to make sure it was tight. If either the seal or the bag was damaged in any way, the banks would not accept the delivery. Then he compared the amounts written on the tags at the top of the bags with the amounts on the bank's manifest. One bag had contained $800,000, and the other had contained $400,000.

"Having signed the receipt for the one-point-two million, what did you do with the two bags?" asked prosecutor Casey.

"I went back to the truck and I put them in a yellow tub that was in the truck. I put the two bags in the yellow tub."

He said his partner then checked the bags again.

"I was standing on the platform. He checked the two bags. He came back out."

"Out of where?"

"Out of the truck. Locked the doors. . . ."

"Who was it that locked the doors?"

"Bill Proctor."

"Did you see him do that?"

"Yes."

"Can you describe the process of locking the doors?"

"They have a handle on the door that you have to go— you pull up and then down, and two prongs go into the top of the truck and the bottom of the truck, and you press a button in the center and that locks the handle from moving."

"What about the tub? Is there any lock on the tub inside of the truck?"

"No, there was no lock on the tub."

Saracino said he and Proctor then boarded the cab of the truck and drove away from the bank. They drove around the block and then down Arch Street to Delaware Avenue, which runs along the river. They turned right on Wolf Street, and then left on Swanson. "It has a lot of big holes, a lot of bumps. It's a rough road," he said.

"Were you driving the truck, Mr. Saracino?"

"Yes, sir."

"Okay, tell us what happened, if anything, once you got to the Purolator lot."

"We pulled into the first Purolator lot. They let us in the first gate. We came up to open the second garage door. We pulled in and a dispatcher came out and said our back door was open."

Saracino then told how he and Proctor, panicked, reversed the truck and drove back up Swanson Street to find the empty yellow tub. Casey walked Saracino through extended procedural questioning, and concluded with the odd formality of the criminal courtroom.

"I ask you, Mr. Saracino, did you give the defendant seated in the middle of counsel permission to take those two bags?"

Joey looked up. He had been slumped in his chair, looking bored, doodling on a yellow legal pad. He was conspicuously dressed in a silky pink shirt and a tan sport coat and resisted the urge to wink at the driver.

"No, sir," said Saracino.

"Did you give the defendant permission to keep those two bags?"

"No, sir."

"Did you give the defendant permission to use the contents of those two bags in any fashion for any length of time?"

"No, sir."

"After this incident, sir, what happened with regard to your employment?"

"We were fired."

Saracino was cross-examined along the same lines, and then Proctor took the stand. He told the same story. Casey concluded with the same litany, asking Proctor if he gave permission for Joey to take the money.

"No, sir, I did not," said Proctor.

"Did this defendant, to your personal knowledge, ever make any efforts to return those two bags of money to you?"

"No, sir. He did not."

Casey asked about his job.

"Well, we were terminated," said Proctor. "First we were put on an indefinite suspension. Approximately three weeks or two weeks later we got a notice of termination."

In his cross-examination of both men, Kane did his best to deflect any blame Joey may have shared for them losing their jobs. A key to Kane's strategy was to make the episode out to be, as much as possible, a victimless crime. He stressed with both guards that they had failed to properly lock the doors on the truck and so had earned their own dismissals.

When Charles Strebeck, a Purolator executive, testified to the company's loss, which he said was $196,400, Kane asked: "I presume, therefore, Purolator is not insured, is that correct?"

Casey objected, and the two lawyers set to arguing. Casey wondered about the relevance of Purolator's insurance status.

"The relevancy is that if they are made whole, they have the wrong complainant here. . . . Purolator may not have lost anything. If they didn't lose anything, then they are not a victim."

"I have difficulty, Mr. Kane, in seeing the logic of your argument. This is a theft and a crime which is being alleged, then the complainant is the Commonwealth. Period."

"Okay . . . ," said Kane. "But I think the jury has a right to know if this victim is in fact a victim to the extent that we're painting him. He is up there saying, 'Judge, we're out $196,400.' He is not out $196,400."

Judge Chiovero ruled against him. On further cross-examination, Kane brought out that reward money had been paid to Jed Pennock, John Behlau, Mike DiCriscio, and John DiBruno. Not only was no one hurt, Kane's questioning implied, Joey's caper had actually left a trail of happy money in its wake. Kane also got Strebeck to confirm that the guards had improperly locked the doors of the truck

"As a result of your investigation, you fired the two drivers?" he asked.

"That's correct," said Strebeck. "Our investigation revealed that the door and the lock were in proper working order."

Kane could feel reasonably good at the end of the first day. The prosecution's effort to show that Joey's "crime" was not victimless had been reasonably well checked, and Jed Pennock, who had begun his testimony shortly before the trial was adjourned for the evening, had unexpectedly handed Joey and his lawyer a gift. Under direct examination, testifying for the prosecution, Jed was asked by Casey, "When you saw the defendant Friday night, . . . did you talk about the reward?"

"Yes, we told him there was a reward."

"What was his response, if anything, to your suggestions concerning the reward?"

"No response."

"He said nothing?"

"No."

"What was his reaction without saying what he said?"

"He was going crazy," Pennock said. That got everybody's attention, as Joey was offering an insanity defense. Finding the money, he was claiming, had driven him temporarily insane. Pennock was the prosecution's first big witness, and he was already making Joey's case.

"What do you mean by 'crazy?'" asked Casey, attempting to regroup.

"He said he wanted to keep the money, that he didn't have the money and stuff like that, and he was slamming his hands on the table."

That exchange had taken place just minutes before Judge Chiovero closed things down for the day. Kane couldn't have scripted a better idea to leave with the jurors on their first night of sequestration.

4

Kane picked right up with that theme when he began questioning Jed the next morning, walking him through the moment when they'd found the money.

"When you saw the money, what happened in the car?" Kane asked. "Did everybody get excited?"

"Yes, very excited," said Jed.

"Everybody started jumping up and down and kissing each other?"

"Yes, hugging each other."

"Everybody went crazy?"

"Yes."

Later, when he reviewed Jed's account of Joey's response to the suggestion of going for the reward, Kane drove the point home.

"And you said Joey went crazy . . ."

"Yes."

"You told him to return the money, and Joey wouldn't listen to you?"

"He wouldn't listen."

"He wouldn't listen to reason, would he?"

"No. He was too upset that he had all that money and he wanted to keep it."

"He was too excited about the money?"

"Yes."

"And he just wanted to keep it?"

"He was all excited."

"And he wouldn't listen to reason, is that correct?"

At this point, Casey objected.

"It's a phraseology," said Kane, speciously.

"A lot of people don't listen to reason," Casey said.

The judge allowed Kane to continue.

"You said he was too upset?"

"Yes."

"And he was too excited?'

"Right."

"And he was running around jumping up and down; isn't that correct?"

"Yes."

"And he was acting like a nut; isn't that correct?"

"Objection, your honor," interjected Casey again.

"I think that phraseology is common," said Kane.

The judge asked Jed if he understood what Kane meant by the word "nut."

"Yes," said Jed.

"What does that word mean to you?" the judge asked.

"It means that he was out of control of himself, sort of."

Kane was loving this.

"All right," said the judge. "You may answer the question."

"Is that what he was acting like?" asked Kane.

"Yes."

"He was totally out of control of himself?"

"Yes."

"And you couldn't reason with him nor could Masi or Behlau?"

"That's correct."

"And you tried?"

"Yes."

Kane continued in this vein, taking advantage of every opportunity that presented itself to elicit Jed's opinion that Joey was acting "crazy," "out of control," that there was "no reasoning with him." Casey got a chance to address this on redirect. If Kane was going to pile on this glib diagnosis of Joey's insanity, Casey was going to at least clarify terms. Only the effort backfired on him.

"Did Mr. Coyle recognize the hundred-dollar bills to be hundred-dollar bills?" he asked.

"Yes," said Jed.

"Objection, your honor," said Kane. "It's beyond the scope."

"I thought we had some testimony about, I think the word was 'nuts.' I want to see how out of control he was."

But the judge was on a roll as far as Kane was concerned.

"I think that the objection should be sustained for another reason," Chiovero said. "Whether or not Mr. Coyle recognized the bills as hundred-dollar bills, I don't think he [Jed] has any way of knowing."

"Very well," said Casey. Then, turning back to Jed, he asked, "How did Mr. Coyle react upon seeing what *you* recognized to be hundred-dollar bills?"

"How did he act?" asked Jed.

"Yes, sir."

"He was going bananas."

This was not what the prosecutor had in mind. How many slang terms were there for temporary insanity? Casey tried to recover.

"Was there any indication that he thought it was bananas or apples in the bag?"

"No."

"Can you explain whether or not your observations of Mr. Coyle led you to believe he knew where he was at the time?"

"At the time when we found the money?"

"Yes, throughout the time you saw him for the next two days."

"Yes."

"And do you have any reason to tell the jury that he didn't know who he was or where he was?"

"The only time I think he didn't know where he was, was, like, Friday night."

"On Friday night, what led you to the conclusion that he didn't know where he was?"

"Because he was going crazy, slamming his hand on the table and stuff."

"Do you think he knew where the table was when he went to slam his hand?"

"Yes."

There. Casey had established that Joey Coyle was sufficiently sane to know how to bang his fist on a table. This was not going well. Casey had to do something. Since Kane had effectively raised the issue of insanity already, the prosecutor decided to ask Jed about Joey's drug use. Under the law, if Joey's actions were the result of being high, then they could not be ruled insane.

"You have seen the defendant on many occasions before the time he looked nuts to you, right?" Casey asked.

"Yes."

"Now, have you also had occasion to see people under the influence of methamphetamine?"

Kane shot up from his chair.

"Objection, your honor!"

"Sustained," said the judge.

"I am going to elicit an opinion," said Casey.

This prompted a long argument before the bench, out of the jury's earshot. Casey argued that if Kane was using an insanity defense, he should be able to show that Joey's erratic behavior was more likely the result of his drug use.

"If not knowing right from wrong is from drug use, it is not legal insanity," whispered Casey.

"There has been no testimony as to methamphetamine . . . ," said Kane. "There is no report in evidence."

"Not yet," said Casey. "Let's not play games. It's there."

"The doctor is not going to say he was using methamphetamine," said Kane. "He said he used methamphetamine, that's all he said. He did not say he was using it at this time. That's not in this case."

"I have to be able to prove that it is not mental illness, which is somebody who is on drugs, which is not legal insanity," Casey told the judge.

"This person is not qualified in the first place to render an opinion as to whether somebody's under the influence of methamphetamine, absolutely not qualified," said the judge.

"Who is?" asked Casey.

"An expert on the use of drugs or a doctor, but not this individual."

"Can I do alcohol?"

"Yes," said the judge.

"Why not drugs?"

"He is not qualified to do that."

So Casey was stuck. Jed Pennock had laid a nice foundation for Joey's insanity defense, and there was nothing he could do about it. So Casey gave it one more shot. He prevailed upon the judge to call a recess, and the lawyers huddled with the judge in his chambers for ten minutes. When they emerged, Casey appeared to have won a small victory. Judge Chiovero told the reassembled jury, "As a result of a sidebar conference, I have advised the assistant district attorney that he would be permitted to ask a question of Mr. Pennock whether or not Mr. Coyle, when he was behaving in the manner described as 'nuts,' et cetera, appeared to be under the influence of alcohol or anything of that nature, and that the assistant district attorney must specifically follow that question with, 'Please answer yes or no.'"

"I object," said Kane.

"Mr. Kane objects," acknowledged the judge, who then directed Casey to ask his final question.

Jed retook his seat in the witness box, and Casey stood. The moment had been invested with considerable drama. At best, Casey would get to plant the idea in the jury's mind that Joey was not insane but under the influence.

"Mr. Pennock, at the time that the defendant was acting nuts, as you have described, did he appear to be intoxicated or under the influence of alcohol or something like that? Will you please just say yes or no?"

"No," said Jed.

Which is why attorneys are advised never to ask a question in open court unless they know what the answer will be. Score another victory for the defense.

The questioning of John Behlau followed immediately, and was uneventful, although Casey did manage to inject at least the idea that Joey's befuddlement was self-inflicted.

"At the time that the defendant acted high-tempered and banged his watch . . . did the defendant appear to be intoxicated or under the influence of alcohol or anything like that? Would you tell me yes or no?"

"Yes," said Behlau.

But that was all the judge would allow. Casey concluded his case by calling Linda Rutter, the frail nineteen-year-old woman who defined the term "mousy." Her blond hair hung limp to her shoulders. Linda was so frightened by the court and so upset that she was being called as a witness against Joey that, during just the preliminary questions to establish her name, address, and relationship to the case, she began to shake in the witness box and then broke down in tears.

"Try to compose yourself," said the judge, kindly. "Try to relax. I know it is difficult under these circumstances."

Linda came back reasonably composed after a five-minute break and fielded a spate of routine questions. Then Casey once more zeroed in on the drug issue.

"Now, Miss Rutter. Can you estimate approximately how much time you spent with the defendant during that whole period?" he asked.

Linda looked blank.

"Just estimate. If you can."

"About three days," she said.

"During that time you were with him, was the defendant using drugs at all?"

"Objection," said Kane.

"Sustained," said the judge, who was clearly growing weary of this.

"Do you know what drugs are?" Casey asked Linda.

"Objection," said Kane.

"Sustained," said the judge.

This prompted another conference in the judge's chambers.

"Your honor, the witness will be able to testify as an eyewitness to seeing the defendant use a needle to shoot up what apparently was drugs on more than one occasion throughout the time period during which his state of mind, namely insanity, is being raised by the defense."

Kane argued that bringing up testimony of Joey's drug use was simply a way of prejudicing the jury against him, and that Joey's drug use had no bearing on the charges against him.

"It is prior crimes," said Kane. "He is introducing prior crimes not to show any plan, scheme, or design. Okay? Clearly that's exactly what he is doing. The prejudice here is clearly indicated. The only reason he wants to bring this in is to prejudice the jury."

Judge Chiovero ruled against the prosecutor, so Casey was unable to use Rutter to establish that Joey had been on a drug and alcohol binge from the first hours after he'd found the money. To make matters worse, in cross-examination, Kane got Rutter to hammer home even further his claim that Joey was temporarily insane.

"Now, that Monday, when he went to the shopping mall, did he seem very confused to you that day?" Kane asked her.

"Yes."

"Did he seem irrational to you that day?"

"Yes."

"Did he seem bizarre to you that day?"

"Yes."

"He made a phone call from the mall, is that correct?"

"He never really got to make it, but he began to dial a number."

"Somebody from the telephone company came and went into the next phone booth?"

"Yes."

"Joey thought he was an undercover somebody or other, is that correct?"

"Yes."

"Did you think that was funny?"

"No, not at the time."

"He was quite frightened at that time, wasn't he?"

"Yes."

"He was paranoid at that time?"

"Yes."

Later, when Linda said she thought Joey was "not playing with a full deck" and the defense attorney asked for her to elaborate, it prompted an extended exchange between Casey and Kane at the judge's bench over whether she was qualified to make such a judgment.

"A lay person can give you her observations," Casey said, "she can tell you how crazy he looked, but she cannot give you the ultimate issue that the jury has to find: Did he know what he was doing? Did he know it was wrong? This is for the jury to decide."

"I think you can elicit the information that you require without asking her directly whether or not he, in her opinion, knew what he was doing," the judge told Kane. "Can you do that?"

"I guess I can, sure," said the defense attorney.

Kane went on to ask Linda, "When he wasn't 'playing with a full deck,' do you mean he wasn't balanced?"

"Yes."

"Unbalanced, would that classify it?"

"Yes."

"Irrational?"

"Yes."

"Out of control?"

"Yes."

"Did he look like he didn't want to ever have this money?"

"Yes."

"He was sorry that he ever found this money?"

"Yes."

Not long after that, Casey rested his case. With the judge's help, Kane had run circles around him. The trial adjourned for the weekend. On Monday, the defense attorney would present Joey's case.

5

rank Santos took the stand first on Monday. He might just as easily have been called as a witness for the prosecution, given that he had spent several days trying to help Joey flee the country with the fraction of the money he had left. But once Frank got started it was easy to see why Casey hadn't done so. Joey's old friend was tenacious in his defense, arguing that Joey had been thrown so off balance by his discovery of the money that he was behaving like a child. Of course, Frank didn't mention that Joey was flying high on speed.

"Now, on the way to New York I was trying to explain to Joey what the law is," he said. "I knew what the law was as far as money was concerned. Finders keepers is an old common law. . . . I couldn't get through to him that the money was not his, that everybody involved would have to give the money back."

"So, in other words. When you say you were trying to get through to him, he didn't understand that?" asked Kane.

"He didn't understand that. Joey believed in the old common law, finders keepers, losers weepers. All Joey knew was he found the money and it was his and everybody he gave the money to. . . . He didn't understand it. Never did."

Frank said that the only time during the whole episode when he saw Joey calm was after they'd been arrested. "He was kind of relieved," he said.

"That he didn't have the money any longer?" asked Kane.

"The first time I seen him sleep."

"How would you characterize Joey's behavior of March third and March fourth?"

"Paranoid, erratic. He was like a little kid. He didn't understand the things that he would have understood, like, maybe a year ago. I mean, he couldn't even remember my own mother's name, my own birthday. He has been over to my house numerous times and he couldn't remember the address. I have known him a long time. I grew up with the guy and he was a completely different person."

"Would you say he was nuts?"

"Nuts, crazy. He is bananas all right."

This drew chuckles in the courtroom. Joey smiled gamely.

"Was he at any time during this period rational, in your opinion?" Kane asked.

"In my opinion, no."

"In your opinion, was he out of control?"

"He was crazy. He was definitely crazy, all right."

Casey did his best to counter this buddy-buddy routine. Wasn't it a coincidence, he noted, that of all Joey's friends he went for help in his "crazy," "irrational" state to the one friend who helped steer ships in and out of Philadelphia, or whose wife was a travel agent?

"Ex-wife," said Frank.

"Now, the defendant had already decided before he met with you that he was going to get out of the country; isn't that a fact?"

"No, sir."

"It's your testimony that it was completely your idea for him to get out of the country?"

"Yes, sir."

"He didn't talk to you about, 'I'm going to go to Ireland'? or 'I'm going to get out of here and go to Italy'? He never told you that, right?"

"No, he did not."

He was lying to help his friend. Joey had talked about leaving the country well before he had hooked up with Frank, and had proposed it to him. Casey wasn't getting anywhere. He shifted gears. He asked why Frank had chosen Mexico as a destination. Frank said it was because you didn't need a passport to travel there, and that Joey didn't want to wait the two days it would have taken to get one.

"By that time, he thought they would have got him," Frank said.

"*They* would have got him?"

"The people chasing him. The guy was hysterical, Mr. Casey."

"Did you see people chasing him?"

"No."

"Is it your testimony that you honestly believe that he was in fear of people chasing him?"

In this, Frank was correct. Joey did have those fears, and they were not unfounded. People *were* chasing him.

"Mr. Casey, you could pick up the newspaper every day and read about people getting killed for ten dollars, twenty dollars. What do you think they would have done to him for one hundred thousand dollars? . . . I believe there was people chasing him."

Casey's frustration with the witness began to show. He decided to hammer at the heart of Frank's testimony, to at least expose his underlying intent.

"You understood clearly before you testified today that insanity was the issue and you had to convince the jury that he didn't know what he was doing? You understood that before you came in here today, didn't you?"

"Repeat that again, please."

"Okay, I will give you some time to think about it."

"No. Repeat it, please," asked Frank.

The question was read back by the court stenographer.

"My understanding was to tell the truth about Joey's behavior," said Frank.

"Let's make it clear," said Casey. "Are you going to tell the jury now that you didn't understand that you were being called as a witness to show that he didn't know what he was doing?"

"I understood that I was being called as a witness."

"And not why?"

"Yes. Why? Because I was with him."

"Not to the issue of insanity?"

"I am not up here—I am up here to tell the truth, Mr. Casey."

Casey pressed on, but it was clear he was going to get nowhere with Frank Santos. Kane objected when the prosecutor rephrased the question. "I believe he already answered, your honor. He said, 'I was up here to tell the truth.'"

"I don't want him to testify any longer," said Casey, exasperated.

Next up was Joey's sister, Ellen O'Brien, who continued to build the case for Joey's erratic behavior. The very things that had most worried her about him, his impulsiveness, unpredictability, irrationality, now rallied to his defense. She told the jury that her brother had experienced epileptic seizures as a child, and that his craziness after finding the money reminded her of a childhood seizure. She talked about how he thought their father had put the money there for him, and she said she had never seen him so upset and "hysterical." Casey's questioning of Ellen was gentle and did nothing to shake her impressions of him.

Joey fell asleep during her testimony. His head lolled back over the chair.

"Mrs. O'Brien, excuse me." said the judge. I'm sorry to interrupt the testimony at this time. We'll take a ten-minute recess."

The jury filed out. Then the judge explained.

"I asked that the jury be excused from the courtroom, Mr. Kane, because the defendant's head was way back over the chair and he was asleep, and I was afraid that some of the jurors might observe that and it would prejudice them. . . . If the jury sees him in that condition, they'll think he doesn't give a damn about the trial."

Joey was still sound asleep. He was rocking back and forth gently in his chair. Kane woke him up and took him for a walk up and down the hallway.

6

Half the battle of proving that Joey had been driven temporarily insane by his lucky find was won. Since Casey wasn't allowed to elicit testimony of Joey's methamphetamine use, insanity seemed the best explanation for the stories of his manic, sleepless, paranoid behavior. But to seal the argument Kane had to produce a bona fide expert to say so in clinical terms. On Monday morning, March 1, the defense lawyer called to the stand Albert Levitt, a Temple University psychologist who had been asked to examine Joey several months after his arrest. The psychologist was often employed by the courts to examine defendants, to determine if they were fit to stand trial. He had taken the day off from work to come to court to testify for Joey's defense.

He showed the results of simple drawing tests, IQ tests, and inkblot tests to the jury, explained Joey's history of seizures as a child, his inability to hold a steady job, his periods of manic behavior, and described a certain tendency toward grandiosity —"It means that he overvalues or overrates his capabilities." Joey displayed average intelligence but an inability to control his impulses, Levitt said.

"Were you able to arrive at an opinion of the psychological condition of the defendant at the time of this incident?" asked Kane.

"Yes."

"What is that opinion?"

"My opinion was that he was insane."

"Would you go on and explain upon what you base that opinion?"

"I base that opinion on the fact that he was extremely disturbed at the time I tested him, and I extrapolated back to when he found the money. It was such a shock that he couldn't —he went into a frenzy, into a manic phase where he couldn't organize or think clearly or make a decision or figure out right from wrong, and as a result of that I feel that he was insane at the time he had the money in his possession."

"Now, you mentioned the manic condition, that he was thrown into a manic condition. Can you describe that to the jury?" asked Kane.

"'Manic' is taken from the Greek word that means 'frenzy.' A man that is in euphoria, all his feelings are hyper, all his thinking is running a mile a minute, and he can't organize or perceive or think clearly, so that he can't make appropriate decisions and can't make appropriate judgments. And he has a need to make contact with everybody and give things to everybody and run around and take flight, run from the situation, and do all kinds of things that he wouldn't normally do. I don't know that he has ever been normal, but what a normal person would do."

Casey listened to this and thought it aptly described someone high as a kite on speed.

"For this person to get a shock of a million dollars, to come into a million dollars, was probably the worst possible thing that could happen to him, because it tipped him into a psychotic condition, and while he had that money he could not think adequately or clearly," said Levitt.

Casey knew he wasn't going to get Levitt to change his opinion during cross-examination, but he posed one long question that he hoped would undercut the psychologist's conclusion of insanity. The prosecutor walked through all of the very coherent steps Joey took to hide the fact that he had found the money—swearing his companions to secrecy, burning the bags, cellophane wrappers, and tags, hiding the Behlau car in New Jersey—and to escape, by his contacting Frank Santos, dyeing his hair, shaving his mustache, wearing sunglasses, buying the tickets to Acapulco, going to the airport.

"Now, assuming those facts, would that change your opinion as to whether or not the individual was manic?" Casey asked.

"No," said Levitt. "It would heighten it."

"It would heighten it?"

"Yes, because he was doing many, many things and he couldn't decide on what to do that made any sense. He was running around like a lunatic. He was trying to change his identity. Identity change is typical of manic individuals. They take on many names, they take on characterizations, they take on disguises. That's more typical of manic than not."

"You have had a great deal of experience in your position here with the Court of Common Pleas with criminals, have you not?" asked Casey.

"Yes."

"Wouldn't you say that it's pretty average for a criminal, say in a robbery or any kind of crime in which they are sought by the police, to exhibit their consciousness of guilt by flight?"

"Yes. But they are different kinds of crimes than this one. This is a question of—he didn't know whether he was committing a crime or not. He was somewhat delusional. He thought God and his father had something to do with his getting the money. He wasn't sure whether he should give the money back. He was very confused as to whether he was doing something criminal or not."

Casey tried to plant some doubt about Levitt's testing methods, but the phychologist left the stand having made the desired impression on the jury. Next, Kane called Dr. Kenneth Kool, the psychiatrist who had examined Joey soon after his arrest. Kool offered much the same opinion as Levitt. "I see this as a psychiatric case, not a criminal case," he said. Finding the money had temporarily given Joey the delusion that he was "King Coyle," and in that state he was no longer capable of discerning right from wrong.

On cross-examination, Casey took one more stab at getting evidence of Joey's drug addiction into the open.

"Was there any sort of blood tests requested by you for this defendant?"

"No."

"Now, a blood test, of course, would show if there was any sign of alcohol, isn't that true?"

"Yes."

"Did you do or request any urinalysis of the defendant?"

"No."

"Were you to have submitted a urinalysis to a laboratory, it is conceivable or it is possible that they would be able to determine whether or not the defendant was a drug user; isn't that correct?"

"Yes."

Kane objected, and the judge this time allowed Casey to continue.

"Would it be fair to say that the reason you would do such a physical examination would be to first take away any factors, any physical factors, that would be determined scientifically and eliminate them before you go and look for a mental disease that can't be tested scientifically, would that be fair to say?"

Kool said that taking such steps would have been ideal, but that they are not always followed in practice.

"So that I understand your definition, would you agree with the following symptoms of mania," asked Casey, and he began to read a list of symptoms associated with meth use. "Marked euphoria, enhanced physical strength and mental capacity, the individual would need little sleep or food, the individual would tend to be very wakeful, alert, with a decreased sense of fatigue, elevation of mood with an increase in initiative, confidence, and ability to concentrate, often elation, euphoria, increase in motor or speech activity? Would they be symptoms—"

"Objection," said Kane. "I would like to know what he is reading from."

This led to another sidebar discussion. Kane argued that it was clear that Casey had read from a list of symptoms associated with an amphetamine high. The judge decided to let the prosecutor pose the question.

Kool said that some of the symptoms on the list could be associated with mania.

"My question, Dr. Kool, was based on the text of 'Pharmacological Basis of Therapeutics,' by Goodman and Gilman," said Casey, and he explained that these were all symptoms of someone injecting speed. "Would you agree with Goodman and Gilman on that subject of the symptoms of the use of methamphetamine?"

"Yes."

"Did you discuss personally with any eyewitnesses to this case whether or not they had seen the defendant using drugs?"

"Objection," said Kane.

"Overruled," said the judge.

"I asked his sister on the telephone about that kind of thing," answered Dr. Kool, "and she indicated to me that she had seen times when she thought Joey was under the influence of something, and that on the day when she saw him he was clearly not under the influence of any such thing. I asked Mr. Coyle if he had any kind of drug that morning, and he denied flatly having had anything that morning. Those are the two that I recall in particular bringing that question up with."

"Of course, you indicated in your report that after the age of twenty-two that the defendant began the use of methamphetamine; isn't that true?"

"Yes."

"Sir, through your experience you know that legal insanity may not be premised upon drug use; isn't that correct?"

"That's correct, I know that."

And that was as far as Casey could get with it. Since the doctor had not sought evidence of Joey's drug use, there was no way to establish it through him. Casey stopped trying. Kane got one more chance to question the doctor, and he used it to establish that if someone manic, like Joey, took a drug like speed, it might have the effect of actually calming him down.

Casey called rebuttal witnesses in the days after this testimony. He put Linda Rutter back on the stand and asked her directly about Joey's drug use.

"Did you see him under the influence of drugs?"

"Yes," she said.

"And can you estimate about how much of the time that you were with him was he under the influence of drugs?"

"About half the time."

"And did you see him using drugs yourself, actually personally see him?"

"Yes."

"Okay."

Kane stood up.

"Now, you didn't see him use any drugs on Thursday, is that correct?" Kane asked Linda.

"Yes."

"And Thursday you said was his worst day? Thursday and Monday?"

"Yes."

"And, as a matter of fact, when he used the drugs, his behavior actually became better. He calmed down, didn't he?"

"Yes."

"So he wasn't as wild or he wasn't as bizarre or frantic or frenzied when the drugs were used?"

"Yes."

"Okay, and you saw him use drugs before?"

"Yes."

"And he was never wild or crazy before?"

"No."

"It was only after he found the money that he became wild and crazy and frenzied and frantic and bizarre, is that correct?"

"Yes."

"The drugs had the ability to actually calm him down?"

"Yes."

Casey had at last scored the point he had been trying all along to get across to the jury, and Kane had effectively countered it. Then the judge weighed in, addressing the jury as the tiny blond witness walked back to her seat.

"You have just heard testimony regarding the use of drugs by Mr. Coyle. You may believe or disbelieve that testimony . . . since you are the fact finders in this case. However, I wish to instruct you and impress upon you that you must not under any circumstances consider the testimony with respect to drugs as an indication that the defendant is of bad character or did something wrong or improper. It would be fundamentally unfair to Mr. Coyle for you to do so, and I caution you and instruct you. You understand. Thank you very much."

One of the rebuttal witnesses Casey called was an expert witness, psychiatrist Dr. Richard Schwartzman, who testified that in his review of the case, Joey had been "concealing evidence, avoiding detection, and trying to take flight."

"He must have known that it was wrong to be taking those actions," Schwartzman said. "An individual who is insane . . . has no criminal intent. They have no free choice. They are indifferent to the threat of punishment. It certainly sounds to me . . . that this man did know what he was doing and knew it was wrong and was taking action to avoid apprehension."

If Casey had had any doubts about how things were going they were dismissed as soon as he finished offering his rebuttal witnesses. A local reporter named Jack Reilly appeared in court saying he had important information about the case to relate to the judge. Reilly insisted that the judge meet with him one on one in chambers, where he announced that one of the jurors had contacted him by phone.

"He did not identify who the juror was," Judge Chiovero told the lawyers after his meeting with the reporter. "The juror told him that the jury had been discussing this case from the first day [which they are forbidden to do], and that in the minds of this juror there was a clear indication that the jurors were not thinking in terms of the guilt of Joey Coyle but merely of the stupidity of some of his actions. They did not consider him to have committed a crime."

Judge Chiovero questioned each juror about the reporter's charges, and each one denied having discussed the case with anyone. There was not enough evidence to declare a mistrial, so Kane and Casey went ahead with closing arguments, and the jury came back promptly with a verdict. Whether or not Reilly's leak had ever occurred, the information it delivered was accurate. The jurors found Joey not guilty.

It was quite a scene. Joey hugged his lawyer, his sister, and slapped high fives with Frank Santos. In the hallways outside the courtroom, jurors lined up to shake his hand and pat him approvingly on the back. Joey gallantly kissed the hands of all the ladies.

Philadelphia was not ready to send to jail a lovable, generous goof who stumbled on a fortune and lacked the civic discipline to return it. One who wasn't surprised was Pat Laurenzi, who watched the proceedings from a distance. Casey had never called him or the other cops who worked the case as witnesses.

"The trial of Joey Coyle was long, drawn out, and unnecessary," Laurenzi said later. "It was nothing more than headline grabbing by the district attorney. It's everybody's fantasy. We all looked like fools when they were finished. Everybody who had a hand in the prosecution came out looking bad."

Joey came out looking good, much better than he ever felt he deserved. He was a folk hero, "The Guy Who Found the Money." He carried the flat lump of lead that had been used to seal the money bags in his pocket, an amusing reminder of what he got out of the whole episode. People never tired of asking him about the still-missing $196,600, and Joey never stopped denying he knew where it went.

"But nobody believes me," he told me once. "Someday I'm gonna walk out my front door with a shovel over my shoulder and see how many people start following me."

EPILOGUE

JOEY, THE MOVIE, AND A SAD ENDING

Joey celebrated his acquittal the usual way. He got high and did his best to stay high. He hustled for money any way he could, then blew it on meth. He went back to disappointing people, most of all himself. He found it harder to just blend in to the scenery, so trouble found him all the more easily. He was arrested for meth possession eight months later, and was in and out of drug treatment and jail in the coming years.

He never completely gave up the dream of cashing in big, in that great hope of every American who has tasted his bite of celebrity—Hollywood. His story seemed like a natural. A genuine urban folk tale. There was lots of movie talk right from the start, and plenty of interest. Harold Kane negotiated more than one deal for his client, with studios and TV producers, but the most that came of them was a quickie version of the tale for a half hour news-entertainment program. Joey made a little option money every time the project changed hands, a few thousand here and there. Screenplays were written and left languishing. Kane had hopes of coproducing a feature film himself, which kept some of the interest at bay.

Seven years went by.

I played a minor role in the story when it broke. As a city reporter for the *Philadelphia Inquirer,* I had spent one cold evening in the alleyway outside Carl Masi's house, watching cops fish around in a trash can on the back porch, stuck in the typical position of a daily newspaper reporter being kept at a safe distance from a developing story, wondering what was going on. By 1986, when I first met Joey, his story was already a distant memory. He hardly ressembled the slender, cocky figure whose face had been everywhere five years earlier. He was pudgy and pale, good-natured but easily distracted, and seemingly incapable of sustained conversation. I struggled with him for weeks to reconstruct an account of the week he had spent on the run, coming back to him again and again, so often that I frustrated him.

Joey did his best to remember, but the years of addiction had taken their toll. It was not until I started finding the others who shared those days with him that the story began coming together. My version of Coyle's story, essentially the one told here, ran as a three-part serial in the *Philadelphia Inquirer Sunday Magazine* in December 1986.

This was the version of the story that would finally land a Hollywood deal. After the series ran, I started getting inquiries from producers. I told them I was willing to sell the rights to the story I'd written, but that I couldn't guarantee the participation of Joey or anyone else involved. The problem with making a film about real people is that real people usually want some control over how they are going to be portrayed on the giant screen to millions of moviegoers. A studio preparing to gamble millions on a project generally won't shoulder the additional risks of libel suits. So before Joey's story could become a movie, most of the principle characters—Joey, his sister Ellen, Detective Laurenzi, and others—would have to sign a release saying they agreed to let the producers do, basically, whatever they wanted with their characters.

Money is usually sufficient to produce a signature in these cases, but Joey was ambivalent about his fame, and Kane had ideas of his own about how the project should proceed. Once I referred the callers to him, I usually never heard from them again.

Disney was different. People there wanted the story badly enough to work at it. They approached the project like a military assault on a well-fortified position. They would try to obtain releases, a studio exec told me in 1991, "but we're prepared to make the movie without them, basing it just on your story and what's in the public record." I sold an option on the story that year, agreed to hire on as a consultant, referred them to Kane, Joey, Laurenzi, and the others, and wished them luck. I never expected a movie to be made.

One by one, the studio obtained releases, from Laurenzi, Frank Santos, and Joey's older brother Billy. They flew Ellen, her husband, and her children out to Los Angeles, where they were wined and dined and treated to Disneyland. They offered the O'Briens $20,000. Ellen signed, prompting a permanent split with Joey, who felt betrayed. By the time Disney approached Kane, the studio had sewed up enough of the project to argue convincingly that the train was about to leave the station with or without Joey's cooperation. Producer Tom Musca and director Ramon Menendez, who had just scored a surprising hit with their film *Stand and Deliver*, were interested. Disney offered Joey $70,000 up front and about 2 percent of the net —which sounds good but is like an open joke in Hollywood; nobody ever sees "net" profits. Kane would be paid as a consultant on the film. He urged his client to accept the deal, pointing out that the movie was going to be made anyway, and Joey signed.

When Musca and Menendez visited Philadelphia later that year, they still weren't completely sold on the project. Musca was more interested. He had grown up in northern New Jersey before attending film school in Los Angeles, and he liked the idea of capturing on film some of the muscular urban scenery he'd left back east. He envisioned a gritty, cheerful urban parable about greed. Menendez had misgivings. He was a tall, wiry Cuban expatriate with a background in TV journalism and film credits that included first assistant director on Oliver Stone's *Salvador*. He was a social realist who favored projects with a political edge. He was struggling to find some deeper meaning to Joey Coyle's crazy week on the run, something that would justify his commitment of time and energy.

"The problem with this guy is that it sounds like he was just stupid," Menendez said. "You can't build a film around a guy who is just stupid."

If they made the film, both men said, they were determined to adhere as closely as possible to the true story. Of course, that wouldn't be literally possible; the demands of storytelling for film require a tight focus and carefully crafted dramatic narrative. There would be need for deft summarization and some skillfully applied imagination to round out the tale. Before getting to that point, Musca and Menendez had wrestled with broader themes. Was the story of Joey Coyle a comedy or a tragedy, or was it both? Who was the bad guy? Who was the good guy? Who was Joey Coyle? A bumbling Everyman or something else, something with more of an edge? How was he changed by the experience?

In real life, the only change in Joey after the experience was his aura of uncomfortable celebrity. He was a folk hero in Philadelphia, but for all the wrong reasons. Joey was constantly being asked to live up to a larger-than-life image that bore little resemblance to reality.

The producer and director finally agreed to accept the project. Musca saw it as a comedy. Menendez saw it is a window on a larger social problem, the declining industrial base and the loss of blue-collar jobs in the northeast. Joey would be a lovable victim offered a sudden, irresistible way out. My own role was minimal. Technically, I was a consultant, but there was no real consultation. When I did offer suggestions, they were ignored. Everyone was nice to me—they even named a TV reporter in the film after my mother, Lois Bowden—and I was invited to watch on the set one day, but the film was going to go off in its own direction. I had no objection. The story I had written was my take on Joey's experience. The movie was going to belong to the filmmakers.

One thing that Joey was not going to be in the film was a drug addict. In one of my first conversations with Disney executives, before Musca and Menendez got involved, I faced one of those clichéd Hollywood moments. I was asked, "Tell me what this story is about in one sentence."

The phone call had pulled me away from the dinner table, and I sat in my office trying to think fast.

"It's a story about addiction, about the belief that there is a shortcut to true happiness."

There was silence on the other end of the phone.

"No way," the executive said.

I tried to explain. Joey had what therapists would call "an addictive personality." His obsessive, ultimately self-destructive desire to keep the money mirrored his drug addiction. The money was a symbol of the drug. How could you tell the story of Joey Coyle without portraying his meth habit?

"Everybody will hate him," the executive said.

Later, Musca explained it in more detail:

"That was one of the early and more simple choices. I mean, we talked about it. If we were making a very low-budget, shoestring film we might have opted for something more raw. But when you're working for a studio, if you plan to release a film with a large number of prints in broad distribution, you have to go out with the expectation of a return on your investment."

In other words, the great middle-American moviegoing audience was not going to plunk down seven bucks on a Friday night to watch Joey Coyle inject himself with meth. Joey would have to be an attractive person, someone normal people would enjoy watching on screen. Even so, Menendez was dead set against turning the film into a chipper, forgettable Disney-style comedy. He was aiming for more of a black comedy, something hip, humor with a punch. He wanted to use the story of

Joey Coyle to capture, visually and thematically, the desperation of blue-collar America. The character in the movie had to
have a little desperation, and a lot of charm.

When John Cusack came to Philadelphia in October
1992, he was already trying to figure out how to make Joey
hip. Cusack had charm to burn. He had a long string of film
credits for an actor in his mid-twenties—Rob Reiner's *The Sure
Thing,* the delightful cult favorite *Say Anything,* and, more recently,
The Grifters, which had made him a bankable leading man. When
you sign a rising star like Cusack, you have to be prepared to
give him leeway, creative input. Cusack's career in the years since
has remained strong, but it has ebbed and flowed. In 1992,
though, he was hot. Like all young actors who suddenly, inex-
plicably ignite, he was believed to possess at that moment a true
sense of that ineffable, fleeting, essential quality—*what audiences
want right now!* The fimmakers would have been fools not to listen to John Cusack.

As I showed him around various places in South Philly,
stopping by bars that Joey had frequented, walking down the
street where he had found the money, it was clear that Cusack
already had an idea of how he wanted to play Joey. He had not
met his true-life counterpart yet, but he was excited about the
role. Cusack has a leftist political bent, and he liked Menendez's
concept of Joey as a blue-collar victim of heartless, shifting
industrial priorities.

"Their way of life is eroding," Cusack explained. "They
were raised to go to work out on the docks like their fathers
and uncles and older brothers, only there's no work for them

on the docks anymore, and there's nothing else they know how to do."

Cusack had his own twist on all this. A hot topic just then was "Generation X," otherwise known as "slackers," shiftless members of Cusack's age group who were educated, smart, hip, cynical, and jobless. Joey was only one of those things, jobless, but Cusack said he wanted to capture some of that generational angst in his portrayal, the idea of being stuck in adolescence, twenty-eight years old and still living with parents. We talked about Joey at length, and John left me with a few of his ideas. He asked me to think about them and get back to him with what I thought. I worked out a few ideas and called him about a week later. He didn't phone back.

In a way, the real story had begun to just complicate matters. The filmmakers had discovered the same problem Joey himself wrestled with—he did not fit the story. He was not the lovable, simple, charming character the story seemed to want him to be. He was complex, dark, troubled, and addicted.

The actor met his real-life counterpart for the first time in November 1992, on a return trip to Philadelphia. Cusack stopped by the house where Joey was living with his girlfriend, Tish Konowal (the romance with Linda Rutter had fizzled, and she had died of an overdose years before). Joey and Tish were excited about the visit.

"We should have food," Tish said.

Joey said he thought Cusack sounded like a Polish name, so Tish set to work making kielbasa. Turns out Cusack is more Irish than Coyle. They had a good laugh about that over the kielbasa. Joey gave the actor a ring that he would wear during the filming, and Cusack asked to see some of Joey's favorite bars. Joey had stopped going into the neighborhood bars a decade ago. He hadn't given up drinking, but folks in the bars were always teasing him about the missing $196,000, and there was always somebody who would start in with what he "shoulda done wit all that money." Joey took Cusack to his favorite sandwich shop instead.

On screen, Joey Coyle would emerge as a unwieldy amalgam of artistic visions. He was Musca's lovable Everyman, Menendez's social victim, and Cusack's slacker. The actor struggled manfully with the task, managing to play it as both comic and tragic, but ultimately he came across as wrong for the role. Cusack was too much the clever suburbanite. He was far too articulate to pass as a tough, street-smart, blue-collar kid, and possessed too much native charm and had too nimble a personality to come across as Menendez's hopelessly trapped, unemployed longshoreman.

"Frank Santos" became a former girlfriend working for an investment firm, played by Debi Mazur. She's the neighborhood girl who has gotten a good education and a white-collar job, leaving Joey behind. She's drawn back to him by the money (which actually makes her a less than sympathetic character), but winds up falling back in love. Joey loses the money, but he gets the girl.

"In the real story, Frankie Santos comes in too late," explained Musca, who cowrote the screenplay with Menendez and Carol Sobieski. "You can't introduce that important a character that late in a two-hour film without confusing the audience. To keep Frank, we would have to invent a way to bring him into the story earlier, because I think you have to establish what Joey's romantic life is like. You can't really flesh out a character without revealing his personal life ... who does he sleep with, or want to sleep with?"

In short, Joey needed a love interest. Frank became Monica —*get it? MONica-MONey?*

Joey's connection with the mob had to be made more innocent, so instead of his working as a bouncer alongside Masi at the Purgatory Club, in the movie Joey turns to an old friend from school, Vinnie (played memorably in the film by the not yet famous Benicio Del Toro). Instead of Joey living alone in the house his mother had recently left, in the movie Joey lives in his old bedroom upstairs, along with a sainted Irish mother and his brother, Billy (played by the man who would later become Tony Soprano, James Gandolfini). Billy assumes some of the role played in real life by Ellen, and in the Hollywood version he steps in at a critical moment to help his younger brother.

The real Coyle family, his brother and two sisters, watched these maneuvers from a distance and with mixed feelings. Musca got a call one day from Joey's sister Theresa. She had not figured at all in the story, so the producer had never met her. He was wary of taking the call. It is not unusual for family members peripheral to the story to feel bitter about being left out.

"I understand you're making a movie about my family," she said.

"Yes," Musca answered, warily.

"And I understand my mother is going to be in it?"

"Yes, and she'll be portrayed as a very loving, honorable woman who is devoted to her family," Musca said, defensively.

"Here's the first thing you have to understand," said Theresa. "My mother was not a nice person."

Well, by God, in this movie she was going to be. Once the changes start, the ball rolls rapidly downhill.

"It's not so much that we as filmmakers are concerned with profitability as with the fact that we know this is how the studio is thinking," said Musca. "We have to create a story true to what we are trying to accomplish, but with enough accessibility to get the green light from the studio. Or else it doesn't get made."

He and Menendez fought to keep what few elements of realism remained. The studio wanted to clean up the language and go for a PG rating, but how do you realistically depict a rough urban setting without raw language? Disney execs would pencil in notes on the script like, "Let's have more fun!" and "Can't we get more humor into this?"

In the end, the movie failed to satisfy anyone. It wasn't humorous enough for Disney, and it wasn't dark enough for Menendez. It had a great cast; in addition to Cusack, Gandolfini, and Del Toro it featured Michael Masden as Laurenzi and Philip Seymour Hoffman in a small role. It was clever in places, and Cusack acted up a storm. But after Disney viewed the final cut of their $11 million investment, their disappointment was palpable.

"And they dropped the movie," said Menendez. "They did some advertising on TV, but there was no big opening in New

York, no billboards. I think they decided that the movie would not be commercially successful and they lost interest in it."

At the end of the film, Joey/Cusack stands in an airport concourse, hands held high in a dramatic shower of hundred-dollar bills. Police surround him, guns drawn.

"*Run!*" shouts Monica.

"Where?" asks Joey.

The gig is up. The wild, weeklong sprint to keep the $1.2 million is over. Joey is trapped, not only by the law but by the more lasting grip of fame. As he's led from the airport, police struggle to keep reporters and Joey's fans from trampling him. Generous Joey. Lovable Joey. Joey the lover, Joey the social victim, Joey the anguished and articulate spokesman for Generation X . . . as the myth went national it gained size and speed.

"It's important not to let the facts get in the way of the truth," said Musca.

In Joey's case, the facts got very tragically in the way, as it turned out. Three weeks before the release of *Money for Nothing*, on August 15, 1993, Joey Coyle wrapped an electric cord arund his neck and hanged himself in the stairwell of his South Philly home.

As PR goes, this was a total meltdown. Part of the modest publicity package planned for the film called for a tour by Joey and John Cusack. "I'm going to make you a god," Cusack had told him. Joey never saw the movie.

The day he killed himself, Joey called Musca and left a message on his machine. He said he hoped the movie was going well and wanted to confirm the date of the private screening they had scheduled. Cusack was supposed to join them, and Joey said he had a gift for the actor—a diamond ring inlaid with the initials they shared.

But Joey was also terrified of the movie, of its release and all the attention it would bring him.

"It was really bothering him," said his girlfriend. "He was so ashamed of the drug addiction. He was worried that the city would fine him, try to take the movie money away from him."

He was paranoid, the way he got whenever he was high, which was most of the time. The movie money had just enabled Joey's addiction, which poverty had actually kept under some semblance of control.

When I last saw Joey, he looked pale, puffy, and old. His face was so soft and pasty that you could barely even make out the scar anymore. He made a show of being excited about the movie, but he didn't have a very good idea of how he would be depicted. "How'm I gonna look?" he asked me, and he seemed genuinely worried about it.

He showed me the framed covers of the three-part magazine story I had written about him hanging on the wall in his basement, but he confessed that he had never been able to get through it.

"I started it a coupla times," he said, apologetically, "but I never got very far. I've never been a reader. My family and friends told me it was real good."